DEC

T0302740

Manfred Mann's Earth Band

in the 1970s

John Van der Kiste

sonicbondpublishing.com

Sonicbond Publishing Limited
www.sonicbondpublishing.co.uk
Email: info@sonicbondpublishing.co.uk

First Published in the United Kingdom 2023
First Published in the United States 2023

British Library Cataloguing in Publication Data:
A Catalogue record for this book is available from the British Library

ISBN 978-1-78952-243-3

Typeset in ITC Garamond & ITC Avant Garde
Printed and bound in England

Graphic design and typesetting: Full Moon Media

DECADES

Manfred Mann's Earth Band
in the 1970s

John Van der Kiste

sonicbondpublishing.com

Would you like to write for Sonicbond Publishing?

At Sonicbond Publishing we are always on the look-out for authors, particularly for our two main series:

On Track. Mixing fact with in depth analysis, the On Track series examines the work of a particular musical artist or group. All genres are considered from easy listening and jazz to 60s soul to 90s pop, via rock and metal.

On Screen. This series looks at the world of film and television. Subjects considered include directors, actors and writers, as well as entire television and film series. As with the On Track series, we balance fact with analysis.

While professional writing experience would, of course, be an advantage the most important qualification is to have real enthusiasm and knowledge of your subject. First-time authors are welcomed, but the ability to write well in English is essential.

Sonicbond Publishing has distribution throughout Europe and North America, and all books are also published in E-book form. Authors will be paid a royalty based on sales of their book.

Further details are available from www.sonicbondpublishing.co.uk.
To contact us, complete the contact form there or
email info@sonicbondpublishing.co.uk

Follow us on social media:
Twitter: https://twitter.com/SonicbondP
Instagram: https://www.instagram.com/sonicbondpublishing_/
Facebook: https://www.facebook.com/SonicbondPublishing/

Linktree QR code:

Acknowledgements

My thanks are due to Kev Hunter, who has been as helpful as ever in supplying several of the images; to Colin Pattenden, Nigel Stanworth and Rob Flanagan of the Manfred Mann's Earth Band Facebook page, for helpful feedback, invaluable sleeve notes accompanying recent reissues, and helpfully answering specific questions put to them in the course of my research; to my old friend Ian Herne, for bringing certain online sites and items to my attention; and above all to my wife Kim, once again an unfailing support during my writing, research and endless hours spent in my study while seeing through yet another project; my ever-supportive publisher Stephen Lambe, and all the editorial team at Sonicbond.

DECADES | Manfred Mann's Earth Band in the 1970s

Contents

Introduction

To a certain extent, the remarkably eclectic, lengthy career of Manfred Mann (the individual, not the band or bands) has mirrored several of the changes that took place in British pop music in its broadest sense. The Mann-Hugg Blues Brothers of the early 1960s became Manfred Mann, the blues and jazz band who turned into a pop group and reluctant purveyor of hit singles (it's a dirty job, but somebody's got to do it), while following its natural inclinations in other musical genres through several personnel changes until disbanding in 1969. The more experimental Manfred Mann Chapter Three was formed in that year and boldly ventured where few others dared to go, but met with scant commercial success and lasted for little more than a year, after which yet another line-up, theoretically Chapter Four, adopted the name of Manfred Mann's Earth Band. With a few resting periods and inevitably many more comings, goings and sometimes returnings with Manfred remaining the sole constant member, as of December 2022, the Earth Band is still in existence. Its greatest success and its most stable line-up were during the 1970s, hence the focus on that period and their work during this time in this book.

As of the time of writing, strange to say, books about the man(n), the groups and various offshoots can be counted on one hand – excluding the book and booklet included in the packaging of two recent CD and DVD retrospective collections. Greg Russo's lovingly researched *Mannerisms*, which stands alone in its field, has been an invaluable source of information on all stages of the musician's career and that of the several bands he has led, as well as the records they made and the various members' recording careers outside Manfred. Roy Bainton's *Talk To Me Baby*, basically an account of The Blues Band and its personnel, is less relevant but still an essential read. So is Tom McGuinness's light-hearted, *So You Want To Be a Rock 'n' Roll Star*, in which the humour conceals more than a little cynical wisdom about the music business from one who has made it his career since the early 1960s. Speaking of all the various members who have played in one Manfred-led line-up or another, it's interesting to observe that none has to date yet committed their memoirs to print, while no other rock journalist has seen fit to look at any of the groups or life and times in the detail they surely deserve, beyond occasional articles in the general and music press.

Above: Manfred Mann's Earth Band (Chris Slade, Manfred, Colin Pattenden, Mick Rogers), at the time of the eponymous debut album, 1972. *(Polydor/Universal Music Group)*

Below: Manfred Mann Chapter Three (Mike Hugg, centre back row beside Manfred). Formed in 1969, they released two albums and disbanded a year later. *(Vertigo/Universal Music Group)*

The 1960s - From jazz and blues to pop and back again

Manfred Sepse Lubowitz was born in Johannesburg, South Africa, on 21 October 1940 and raised in a Jewish family. They always had a piano in the house, initially played by his mother and then from the age of six by Manfred himself, who had demonstrated a keen musical ear from a very early age and would often practise up to five hours a day. After studying classical music at Witwatersrand University, Johannesburg, and working as a jazz pianist in local clubs, he moved to Britain in 1961. He had realised that his career opportunities as a musician and teacher would be far greater there than at home, and he also had a bitter hatred of the apartheid system in South Africa. The country left the British Commonwealth in May of that year, and for a period of 12 months, nationals were allowed to apply for work permits in the United Kingdom.

At first, he taught music and harmony theory, while supplementing his earnings by continuing to perform as a musician, and writing regularly for *Jazz News* under the byline Manfred Manne. He had chosen his alias in homage to noted contemporary jazz drummer Shelly Manne, but soon dropped the final letter. At around the same time, he also joined the Ken Goddard Quartet, a jazz band that had been booked for the 1962 summer season at Butlin's holiday camp, Clacton. He soon became a close friend of another member, Mike Hugg, who was playing vibes. By this time, British trad jazz was rapidly being eclipsed by rhythm and blues, and several musicians in the former field were faced with the prospect of adapting their style if they wanted to continue pursuing a career in an uncertain business. Until then, Manfred had never even heard of Chuck Berry or Bo Diddley, and was listening mainly to the likes of Ornette Coleman, Miles Davis and Thelonious Monk. It soon dawned on him that 'if you did the right kind of Ray Charles, the right kind of Charlie Mingus', and studied what the rock 'n' roll performers were doing as well, that would be way forward.

He and Mike had become close friends, and at the end of the season, they decided to form their own outfit, The Mann-Hugg Quartet, with Mike switching to drums and by the end of that year, they were leading an ensemble comprising Dave Richmond on double bass, and Mike Vickers on guitar. After their first appearance at the Marquee Club in December, they asked the MC, Bob Carey, if he knew of any unsigned singers who might be suitable. He recommended Paul Jones (born Paul Pond), a powerful vocalist and virtuoso on blues harmonica, who had previously played with blues multi-instrumentalist Brian Jones. If events had taken a different course, he might have ended up fronting the band that would shortly become The Rolling Stones, instead of Mick Jagger.

Renaming themselves The Mann-Hugg Blues Brothers, they also recruited three horn players. After residencies at the Marquee, the Crawdaddy and Studio 51 clubs in London, early in 1963, they acquired a manager and a record deal with EMI's HMV label. The three horn players left, as did Dave Richmond, who was replaced on bass by Tom McGuinness. Dave was a first-class jazz bass player, but if they wanted to do a Chuck Berry number or something similar, he was not such a good fit. When they asked Tom if he could play simply, his answer was 'definitely!' What he hadn't told them was that he'd never yet touched a bass guitar in his life, but was confident of his ability to learn on the job – and learn he did very fast.

Their manager Ken Pitt and producer John Burgess both disliked the name Mann-Hugg Blues Brothers, and after everyone was unable to agree on a suitable alternative, he suggested they should call themselves Manfred Mann. None of them, least of all the pianist himself, were completely happy with the change. As a compromise, it was decided that all five individuals should each be known as Manfred Mann. They accepted it at first, though it would later become a cause of friction. As the vocalist, 'the face' and the most conspicuous member of the group, Paul Jones would always resent people greeting him with 'Hello, Manfred'.

Their first single, 'Why Should We Not', released in July 1963, was a jazz instrumental penned by Manfred, and the second, 'Cock-a-Hoop', a 12-bar blues written by Paul, who was featured on vocals and harmonica. It received good reviews in the music press though neither of them charted. Mike Hugg said that at this point, they were still 'very much into the music', with no intention of trying to be commercial or establish an image. They were simply trying to be different and follow their collective inclination as a quintet.

Yet the choice was open to them as to whether they wanted to be a group with minority appeal and risk being dropped by their record label because they failed to sell records, or set their sights on the big time. It would be a case of third time lucky after they were not only invited to appear on ITV's weekly music show *Ready Steady Go*, but also commissioned to write and record a new theme song. The result, '5-4-3-2-1', which was credited jointly to Manfred, Paul and Mike, launched what would be a long list of hits, reaching No. 5 early in 1964.

Another single, 'Hubble Bubble Toil and Trouble', following the same R & B shuffle template and written jointly by all five, narrowly missed the Top 10 that summer. After that, the management persuaded them that something less bluesy and more pop would be more acceptable to the public, and their less than unanimous choice fell on 'Do Wah Diddy', which had been a minor American success for The Exciters earlier that year. Renamed 'Do Wah Diddy Diddy', it may have been a trite, infectious little throwaway, but Paul's spirited vocal and Manfred's distinctive keyboard riffs gave it the right amount of character that lifted it out of the mere bubblegum category. Naggingly commercial, it was the perfect vehicle for their sound. Their version topped the British singles chart for two weeks in August and repeated the feat in America a couple of months later, making them the first British invasion band from southern England to achieve such a feat. Mike Hugg admitted that they 'trimmed the rough edges off it', and despite its success, they were none too happy at finding themselves being turned by EMI into a pop group against their inclinations.

Their nearest competition, perhaps, was in the shape of The Rolling Stones. But while the quintet fronted by Mick Jagger were raw, musically unpolished, cheerfully unkempt and deliberately promoted an uncompromisingly anti-establishment image, Manfred Mann altogether sounded more refined as well as looking much more clean-cut, closer to a more blues-based version of The Beatles.

Like the preceding singles, 'Do Wah Diddy Diddy' was conspicuous by its absence from the British (although not the Canadian) track listing of their debut album, *The Five Faces of Manfred Mann*, released in Britain in September. The sleeve notes carried a subtle allusion to the fact that they didn't see themselves as chartbusting teen fodder; 'their greatest satisfaction is that in spite of their phenomenal success they can still play the kind of music they believe in and carry it to an ever-widening audience.' With five originals (three by Paul Jones, two penned jointly by Paul and Manfred Mann), alongside excellent versions of Julian 'Cannonball' Adderley's 'Sack o' Woe', Joe South's 'Untie Me', and Howlin' Wolf's 'Smokestack Lightning', its predominantly blues, jazz and even soul flavour clearly did not put off buyers. There were even nods to rock 'n' roll in 'Down the Road Apiece', a song written in 1940 by Don Raye but later made famous by Chuck Berry and also covered by The Rolling Stones, and in 'Bring it to Jerome', a number associated mostly with Bo Diddley. It would prove the most successful album of their career, peaking at No. 3.

From then on, group compositions, more often than not instrumentals, would be confined to their B-sides, EPs and albums. Most of the A-sides were cover versions, and despite being infectious pop tunes, rarely less than high quality. They became the first high-profile British act to cover songs by Bob Dylan, whose own albums and singles dominated the charts during 1965, often riding higher in England than in America. Manfred liked Dylan's songs, as to him, they seemed to be commercial without having to conform to the 'moon and June' mindset. Dylan saw the group live in concert, and at a press conference later that year, he praised them for their recordings of his material, saying that 'each one of them has been right in context with what the song was all about'. 'It gave me far more pleasure to hear that than anything else,' was Manfred's response. 'For Dylan to say we do his stuff better than anyone else really is nice.' A bestselling EP by the group in the summer of 1965 featured their take on 'With God on Our Side', the lyrics of which questioned the morality of war and Christianity. A few weeks later, 'If You Gotta Go, Go Now', one of several songs Dylan had written and recorded but not yet released himself, became a No. 2 hit for them in Britain.

Manfred Mann's manager, Ken Pitt, was also Bob Dylan's publicist in London for a while. It was a state of affairs that allowed the group first refusal on some of the latter's not so well known songs as potential singles. History has it that in the early days, Manfred was listening to a few tapes in the office and enquired why Dylan used to choose such a lousy singer to record his demos. He was promptly informed that the 'lousy singer' was the songwriter himself.

In 1971, Manfred was asked what difference a major transatlantic chart record had made to the group. He conceded that they became more successful, but didn't earn much more money. 'We ended up just working a lot more.' They had already been doing reasonably well as a live attraction in Britain, and as a result of topping the American charts, they were invited to tour there, but they did not enjoy the experience and never returned during the decade.

While most of their contemporaries, or perhaps, more importantly, their management and record companies, were keen to consolidate their success across the Atlantic, Manfred took the opposite view. The months of hard graft that would be needed for them to crack the market open would be better spent by concentrating their efforts on the global picture elsewhere. Live shows and television appearances in Britain and Europe, especially Germany, helped to keep them in the public eye, and in October 1965, they became the first British group to play behind the iron curtain in Czechoslovakia. They also had a fan base in the Far East, and included Singapore, Hong Kong and New Zealand on their tours.

As for being hit paraders in their own country, he conceded that it was 'nice to have a No. 1', but he didn't enjoy 'the teenybopper ego trip', and it only lasted a few weeks for him. There was no great pride in achieving recognition for their ability to 'cold-bloodedly string hit singles together'. When a record flopped, they were suddenly no longer flavour of the month. Teenagers were fickle, and audiences suddenly lost interest in them and stopped coming to gigs. In a 1982 interview with Sheridan Morley in *The Times*, Paul said that the group were 'mainly out-of-work jazzmen trying to earn a crust somewhere halfway from jazz to rock', then decided to make compromises towards pop, 'and gradually, the compromises were what we played all the time'. At concerts, they would generally play a medley of their hits early in the act to get them out of the way, and then concentrate on their preferred style. Eric Clapton, like many of their other contemporaries, always believed that Manfred Mann were one of those acts, like The Yardbirds (of whom he was briefly a member) and The Animals, who always sounded far better live than on record.

None of the band really enjoyed playing to younger audiences, who obviously weren't interested in the music and screamed so much that they could barely hear what they were playing onstage. Mike Vickers was the first to decide that he'd had enough and left in 1965 to pursue a more satisfying and creative career in writing, arranging and conducting for movie and TV themes and other artists. Paul Jones told them at around the same time that he was going to give notice as well and would depart once they'd found a suitable replacement, a search that took them about a year. He'd never regarded membership of the group as a long-term career move and, in his words, had more to do with what he saw as the big picture. 'I hadn't joined the band thinking, "Oh, great, I'm in a band,"' he said. '"That's the rest of my life now."'

In January 1966, they were involved in an accident while travelling back to London after a gig at Hull University when their van skidded across a carriageway and collided with a stationary vehicle. Manfred and Paul both sustained injuries, including a broken collarbone and severe bruising. The former recovered quickly, but the latter was out of action for several weeks and unable to sing. Without their vocalist, the remaining members decided to make good use of the time by recording some instrumentals, including jazz-style rearrangements of recent British hits such as 'I Got You Babe', '(I Can't Get No) Satisfaction', 'Still I'm Sad', and 'My Generation', in addition to original material such as 'The Abominable Snowmann' and 'Bare Hugg'. Such material found little favour with their more pop-oriented following but were savoured by a slightly older audience who appreciated the musical experimentation and their foray into another genre.

Other personnel changes saw the brief recruitment and departure of two well-respected jazz horn players: Henry Lowther on trumpet and Lyn Dobson on saxophone and flute. Another musician who joined on a short-term basis was bassist Jack Bruce, who'd formerly been part of John Mayall's Bluesbreakers. He'd given Mayall no warning of his intention to leave, and the latter only learned about it when he saw the news pages in the next issue of *Melody Maker*. John and Eric Clapton, who was in his group at the time, were sufficiently annoyed to sit down and write a new song, 'Double Crossing Time', with a reference in the lyrics to 'double crossing man(n)'. Jack only stayed with them for a few months, but distinguished himself by playing his first gig with the group without a single rehearsal and without one wrong note.

He also remained with them long enough to enjoy a few weeks of top pop glory by playing on the next single. Recorded in March 1966, shortly after Paul Jones had made a full recovery from his injuries, 'Pretty Flamingo' was released a month later and topped the British charts for three weeks, as well as taking them back into the American Top 30 despite their reluctance to undertake a second tour there. Jack left a few weeks later to help form Cream, the first of the 'supergroups', with the evidently forgiving Eric Clapton and drummer Ginger Baker. His replacement was Klaus Voormann, a British-based German player who'd befriended The Beatles during their early days in Hamburg and would subsequently play with George Harrison and John Lennon during their post-Beatles careers. A talented artist, he also designed the sleeves of The Beatles' *Revolver* and the first Bee Gees album.

The departure of Paul Jones left huge boots to fill. To replace him, Manfred and Mike Hugg drew up a list of possible replacements they would like to audition, among them Wayne Fontana, Long John Baldry and the still little-known Rod Stewart, but each one had ongoing commitments already. At length, they spotted Michael d'Abo, the singer and occasional keyboard player with the struggling (and shortly to disband) A Band of Angels. After an audition, he joined in the summer of 1966.

Paul bowed out to pursue a career that embraced recording solo material as well as acting on stage and screen. EMI were sure that Paul Jones as a soloist on the HMV label would be a better commercial proposition, and retained him on their roster. For him, it didn't turn out to be the game-changer he had envisaged at first. 'I left, ended up with the same producer, and recorded other people's songs just as much as I did in Manfred Mann,' he told Alexis Petridis in *The Guardian* in 2021.

The band had been increasingly dissatisfied with EMI's attitude towards them and they moved to the Fontana label, a subsidiary of Philips. To everyone's surprise, not least their own, they would prove the more consistent in chart terms, with seven of their nine subsequent singles making the Top 10 and only one missing the Top 50 altogether. By contrast, Paul would only manage two Top 10 hits, followed by a couple that made the Top 50 and then a string of flops. Two of Manfred's top tenners were Dylan compositions. The first was 'Just Like a Woman', a song from his seminal 1966 double album *Blonde on Blonde*, in which they omitted not only the bridge but also the second verse, with its veiled reference to Queen Mary (amphetamines) just in case including it fell foul of BBC radio and TV. Eighteen months later came the evergreen No. 1 success 'Mighty Quinn', of which the writer's own version was to remain unreleased until a live recording at the Isle of Wight Festival in August 1969 appeared on his *Self Portrait* set the following summer.

Meanwhile, their B-sides, EPs and album tracks, many self-penned, had allowed them to pursue a more adventurous direction. Some of their original songs alternated between psychedelia and music hall, while they also continued to play jazz and blues instrumentals with relish. Manfred and Mike Hugg also composed the soundtrack music for the 1968 movie *Up the Junction*, starring Dennis Waterman in his first major role on screen, as well as a score for *Venus in Furs*, which was billed as an art film but came to be regarded as third-rate soft porn, and several TV commercials.

At around the same time, Manfred acquired and became part owner of a recording studio in Old Kent Road, Maximum Sound, later to be renamed the Workhouse. Having realised that the group was spending so much money in such an environment, he realised that it would make more business sense to acquire his own, or at least one in which he had a share. It was an investment that didn't pay off financially for some time, but creatively it made a difference for the better, especially for his present and future bands. A recording studio, he maintained, was usually a very carefully designed instrument to prevent them from making music. 'We're basically live musicians,' he said. 'We like to play loud, and that causes problems. We like to stand round close together – that's not very easy to do. We like to hear each other without headphones – that can't be done.' To have ready access to somewhere that could be refurbished with such facilities in mind, where they could record in the right setting, would be greatly to their advantage.

Relying on the roller coaster that was the hit parade, being only as popular as their last Top 10 smash, was no guarantee of a stable career in a fickle business. In 1967, a top-five entry 'Ha! Ha! Said the Clown', another infectious but to them irritating little pop ditty, was followed by 'Sweet Pea', an instrumental (written by Tommy Roe, American pop singer of 'Sheila' and 'Dizzy' fame) that only just made the Top 40. Next came a flop (No. 52 in the 'breakers' list), the Randy Newman-penned 'So Long, Dad', ascribed apparently to a manufacturing problem at the pressing plant that resulted in several thousand copies having to be destroyed because of a misplaced hole in the centre and subsequent lack of available stocks to satisfy demand at the right time.

It all came right for them after that with 'Mighty Quinn', which did the complete opposite and gave them a third number one single. Manfred and Mike had been invited to a music publisher's house so they could hear a new batch of songs that Dylan was making available to other artists. The ones that impressed them most were 'This Wheel's on Fire' and 'Mighty Quinn' (at that time, known as 'Quinn the Eskimo'). Mike thought the first would be a better one for them, but Manfred recognised the potential of the second, even though the demo was sung in what he thought was a rambling monotone. As they were not supplied with any printed lyrics, and as Dylan's diction was hard to understand in places, they had to guess at or make up some of the lines. In spite of that, it would remain their proudest achievement of the decade and the song that would become an enduring fixture of the keyboard player's career. In America, it reached number ten, and the group were offered the chance to tour there but decided against it. Fortuitously for them, Paul Jones had also been offered the song to record but turned it down.

The character in the song was said to have been inspired by Anthony Quinn and his starring role as an Eskimo in the 1960 drama movie *The Savage Innocents*. Dylan denied it, saying it was only 'a simple nursery rhyme'.

While they continued to keep the record company happy with hit after hit most of the time, they recognised that with Michael d'Abo as front man they had changed musical direction, and not in the way they would have preferred. With hindsight, Manfred said that they were a good live unit when they were just playing blues. Their second phase in the mid-1960s, he opined, was 'nowhere near as good as the years went by, as it became more of a pop band. In fact, until Manfred Mann's Earth Band, the band with Paul Jones was the best live band.'

As a keyboard player, Manfred was one of the pioneers throughout the 1960s. He became the owner of the first Minimoog in Britain, and was probably the first musician to use a Mellotron on a hit single, namely 'Semi-Detached Suburban Mr James' (originally 'Mr Jones' but altered for obvious reasons), the second of the 45s to feature d'Abo on lead vocal in 1966. In doing so, he narrowly beat The Beatles' groundbreaking 'Strawberry Fields Forever', released early the following year.

Yet they were becoming increasingly disenchanted with the record company's view of them as top 10 fodder, making no secret of their dislike of songs such as 'Ha! Ha! Said the Clown' and their swansong two years later, 'Ragamuffin Man', which Manfred called 'just a little, cute, silly song'. Released in April 1969, it was panned in *Melody Maker* by DJ John Peel, Radio 1's standard-bearer for what was then termed 'underground' music, anything that was the antithesis of commercial pop, as a 'must get into the Top 20' record with no identity. Some years later, Manfred remarked with hindsight that their best material was never the most successful. He thought that *The Five Faces of Manfred Mann* was 'a really good album', as were some of the B-sides. 'I'm not at all putting down what we did, as people imagine, but the best stuff we did was not the hit records.'

None of them wanted to be pin-ups for ever, here today and gone tomorrow, only as good as their last Top 10 entry. Having announced in February 1969 that they weren't going to play live in England any more, a few weeks later, they confirmed that they were splitting up. 'The public was bored with us,' Manfred said. 'They liked the records and people were buying them, but there was no sense of excitement any longer. I think that all of us were more capable in all different ways.'

They had not toured for several months and regarded themselves as a group of musicians making one single after another purely to fulfil their contract. Each of them had realised that there was more to a musical career than looking for the next catchy little tune from outside writers for another smash, and putting considerable effort into a more ambitious album that would probably garner no more than meagre sales. They had already recorded a possible follow-up single, 'Please Mrs Henry', written by Bob Dylan and recorded with The Band with this title during the legendary 1967 'basement tapes' sessions, but it was promptly scrapped and to date has never been legitimately released.

Calling time on a successful group while they were still riding high, and with a record company who were probably waiting eagerly for the next hit after that, was something he'd never regret. As he later told Chris Welch of *Melody Maker*, he was proud of the fact that they stopped while they had a record in the Top 10, 'and not when one failed, or that people had lost interest in us'.

Some years later, he was quite equivocal about what they achieved in the 1960s. In 1977 he told Merrill Shindler of *Rolling Stone* that on looking back, he thought their early hits captured the spirit of the time quite well. 'Mighty Quinn' stood out, although he couldn't say the same of 'Do Wah Diddy Diddy', which was closer to the bubblegum of Ohio Express and their ilk; 'if you put that next to the Beatles' singles, I don't think it stands up.' Two years after that, he mused to a *Sounds* writer the unease he still felt about his former status as a pop star, and about making three-minute singles like 'Ha! Ha! Said The Clown'. 'I felt that there was more in me and it was always a little frustrating to watch other people doing well at music that somewhere inside me, I felt that I could do too. I couldn't do it because it wasn't the right band and because the public wouldn't accept it from you if you did.' The summer of 1969 was time to make the great leap forward.

1970–71 – From Chapter Three to Earth Band

Having been musical brothers in arms from the early days, Manfred and Mike Hugg stayed together for the next couple of years. During the group's final throes, they had formed a new jazz-based outfit, Emanon (just spell it backwards), which played their first gig in London while 'Ragamuffin Man' was still climbing the charts. Once the demise of the old group was made official, Emanon became Manfred Mann Chapter Three. Making a sideways move from Fontana to Philips' new progressive label Vertigo, they spent part of the summer writing and recording new material, and released their eponymous debut album in November 1969.

Chapter Three was a large, rather unwieldy grouping comprising five members plus a five-piece horn section, occasionally augmented in the studio or onstage by backing vocalists Madeline Bell, Linda Lewis and Liza Strike. With so many musicians and roadies on the payroll, the outfit was ultimately too expensive to maintain. Mike moved from drums to piano and vocal, and the group adopted a policy of playing basically freeform jazz-oriented original material with prominent horn arrangements and no permanent lead guitarist. Bass guitarist Steve York contributed six-string guitar (and harmonica) on the debut album, but sparingly. They played live extensively at home and abroad, routinely ignoring calls from the audience to play any of their old hits.

The few records they did release attracted mixed and largely unenthusiastic reviews, as if journalists hardly knew what to make of them but felt obliged to give them at least a guarded welcome. One called the debut album 'an extraordinary album full of the impossible', while another commented on Mike Hugg's voice 'sounding like rather overworked sandpaper, developing through some rather fine brass arrangements into a catastrophic free-for-all'. In some songs, there is the faint hint of a commercial hook creeping through. Yet more often than not, any halfway catchy hooks or other elements are swamped by long instrumental sessions, partly improvised, and different time signatures, which can add interest if used constructively but otherwise give an impression of art for art's sake. In other hands, the songs could work well with sympathetic arrangement. One number written a few years earlier by Mike and his brother Brian, 'You're a Better Man Than I', had been a B-side for The Yardbirds, and also a hit in America for Terry Knight & The Pack, but both versions were far superior to the version that appeared on the first Chapter Three album.

Some writers praised them for their sense of adventure in moving so far away from their old pop style, but others were as baffled as the public by this complete musical about-face. Even in a changing musical climate in which it was becoming acceptable for rock bands to issue albums made up largely of tracks that exceeded the seven-minute barrier, Chapter Three records simply didn't sell. Polydor had released their debut in America but passed on the follow-up as sales had been negligible. The world was not yet ready for them, and only a dedicated following wanted to know.

As Manfred would remark despondently, they were playing the kind of music that rock snobs called jazz, and jazz snobs called rock. It was a case of falling between two stools and pleasing nobody. In hindsight, more recent reviewers have been kinder to them, with a retrospective appraisal in *AllMusic Guide* remarking that 'a swaggering horn section compensates' for any indifferent material, and that the sound is not unlike that of 'a darker, moodier Traffic' but with Manfred on the organ instead of Steve Winwood. To call the albums unlistenable would be doing them a disservice, but they are an acquired taste and many fans of the 1960s material might not care for them.

Giving up the unequal struggle, Manfred Mann Chapter Three went their separate ways in the summer of 1970, staying together just long enough to complete a second album released in October. It had been preceded by their only single, 'Happy Being Me', edited down to four minutes from the album's marathon 16. The result included a jaunty (and concise) brass instrumental break, and was arguably the most commercial number they ever committed to vinyl, but *Record Retailer*'s prediction of a British Top 50 success still proved optimistic. A partially recorded third album, which Manfred later said was 'probably the best', remained in the vaults.

He admitted that Chapter Three had been an over-reaction to the poppiness and commerciality of the old group, and had failed; 'people didn't like the albums enough to buy them', and above all, they 'ran out of creative steam'. Jazz rock or jazz fusion had produced only a small handful of chart-making acts, notably from America, Chicago Transit Authority (soon to become Chicago), and from Britain, Colosseum and Nucleus, the only names who would manage to notch up chart albums at around that time without the benefit of a Top 40 single. The most conspicuous example of all was Blood, Sweat & Tears, and Manfred was annoyed when the media dubbed his band the British B, S & T. It was very much a minority taste as far as the public was concerned, and its main exponents soon had little choice to leave the straitjacket behind and embrace other genres. As the old music business cliché went, 'play jazz and starve'.

One of Manfred's British contemporaries, Roy Wood, would have similar experiences a few years later. Having called time on The Move to form ELO and then left them after just one album to form Wizzard, after the latter split, he assembled the similarly large and wilfully uncommercial jazz-rock Wizzo Band. In 1977 they released one album to unanimously disparaging reviews and negligible sales, and disbanded on the eve of a planned full British tour due to lack of interest, finance and poor ticket sales. One is left with the impression that fans of their previous groups ought to like Manfred Mann Chapter Three and The Wizzo Band as well as admire them for boldly defying expectations in embracing a different musical genre altogether – but that for most listeners it's easier to feel admiration for their efforts than really enjoy them for their own sake.

The end of Manfred Mann, the well-established pop group longing to break out into other directions, had coincided with the rise of British progressive rock. Procol Harum, The Nice (soon to go their separate ways with leader Keith Emerson forming Emerson, Lake & Palmer), Pink Floyd, Jethro Tull and Yes were in the vanguard. Instrumental virtuosity, occasional raids on classical, jazz and folk music, and more diverse, even complex lyrical subject matter avoiding the usual songs about love and romance, were the order of the day. This would turn out to be the obvious direction for Manfred Mann. Having laid Chapter Three to rest, he decided to form a new group, one that was, in a sense Chapter Four in all but name. To the press, he said that he had been trapped in a pop band, and then 'in a kind of jazz thing'. Now his principle was 'to not be trapped, it is to do what you feel is right, so that you don't put yourself within any parameters'.

A more cynical school of thought might suggest that during the previous decade, he and his group had jumped from one bandwagon to another, and that now progressive rock was becoming suitably hip and respectable in Britain, this was the only path for him to follow if he was going to keep up with the times. Something commercially acceptable, yet without appealing solely to the hit singles market, was the aim. Another important factor was the necessity of forming a smaller, more compact band. Chapter Three had been anything but cost-effective, and was an experiment that would not bear repeating on financial grounds alone.

The first musician to join him was Chris Slade, a much-in-demand drummer who had played on several albums for Tom Jones, as well as for Tony Hazzard and Stefan Grossman. More importantly, he had also done a session for the never-completed third Chapter Three album. When asked if he could recommend a bass guitarist, he suggested Colin Pattenden, a friend with whom he had played, who had worked in a similar capacity at various times backing Engelbert Humperdinck, Solomon King and Leapy Lee, and was working in an electronics company at the time. The final musician needed to bring them up to strength was singer and guitarist Mick Rogers, who was born in Essex and worked as a backing musician with Adam Faith and Gene Pitney before going to Australia and playing there with various bands, including Normie Rowe and the Playboys, who were big in their own territory but meant nothing anywhere else. The most notable of these was Procession, who came to England in 1968, where Mike Hugg helped to produce the last album they recorded before splitting up, followed by The Librettos, whose drummer Craig Collinge had been part of Manfred Mann Chapter Three.

When consulted, Mike Hugg gave Mick his unconditional seal of approval. As he was in Australia, Manfred admitted to *Disc & Music Echo* in 1971, it could have been an expensive mistake bringing him over, but fortunately, he turned out to be just the musician he was looking for.

> It was preferable to having to listen to 500,000 guitarists, none of whom would be any good and even if they were, you aren't able to tell good from bad after hearing that many. I have nervous breakdowns about that sort of thing. I really didn't think it was going to work, but we got together for a blow and it did. I don't mean that we all suddenly smiled at each other and it happened, but I'm working with guys I get on with very well and the group, musically, seems very together.

Mick was invited back to England for an audition, and in January 1971, the quartet began jamming together in London. It all came together so quickly that before long, they were rehearsing together and making plans for the future. A few weeks later, they signed to the Philips label for Britain (basically an extension of their existing contract, as Manfred Mann Chapter Three's British releases had been on Vertigo) and the rest of the world except the USA and Canada, where they would join Polydor. The late 1960s band, Manfred ruefully admitted, 'was terrible live', while Chapter Three was inconsistent. Although it was early days yet, at last, he had arrived at the line-up of the best combo he'd ever been involved with.

In those previous bands, Manfred had been noted as a keyboard player, specialising in organ and piano. Now his name was coupled with those of Keith Emerson and Rick Wakeman as one of the first major British wizards of the synthesiser and Minimoog. Manfred had first seen synths being advertised about 18 months previously, and at once, he tried a few but found the small model just as suitable for what he wanted to play, as well as being far less cumbersome. Most of those he saw being offered for sale 'were enormous things with plugs and jack-plugs and computers to pre-set them and thousands of pounds worth of equipment', and while they looked impressive, they offered far more facilities than he really needed. After acquiring the Minimoog, he discovered that he was probably the first player in England to own one. 'I find the instrument very expressive and I don't think that they're gimmick instruments any more, if they're used properly.'

While Emerson and Wakeman had been influenced largely by classical music, Manfred brought more of a jazz feel to his style. He soon became known particularly for his tendency to bend notes downwards on the instrument, a technique he had adapted from listening to Miles Davis, the jazz trumpeter, bandleader and pioneer whose *Bitches Brew*, released in March 1970, was one of the most widely acclaimed and successful contemporary jazz fusion albums. Miles had been recording for almost 20 years, but in around 1968, after listening to James Brown, Jimi Hendrix and Sly and the Family Stone he accordingly modified his technique, in particular abandoning the swing beat in favour of a rock 'n' roll backbeat and more emphasis on bass guitar, as well as plugging his trumpet into electronic effects and pedals like a guitar. To improvised jazz, he and his band added guitar, electronic keyboards and more experimental percussion. By studying and analysing the work of Miles and other jazz fusion pioneers such as Weather Report and Herbie Hancock, Manfred realised there was enormous scope for broadening his style.

During the late 1960s, he had acquired a Hammond organ from The Alan Price Set and customised it extensively. At length, the bottom half housed part of the synthesiser, while the organ itself had been modified to give it a dirty, gutsier tone. Through trial and error, he found out that playing it through ordinary amp stacks, instead of the Leslie speakers that most other Hammond owners relied on, the grimy tone that he was looking for was accentuated. The Minimoog was a smaller version of the one that Keith Emerson had started using onstage once it became apparent that his first instrument of choice was too large to be practical.

Having played piano from an early age, he was quick to appreciate the advantages offered by the new electronic instrument. According to a *Sounds* interview in 1972, as a keyboard player, he always felt a sense of frustration first with the piano, despite the physical connection with it, and then even more with the organ.

> In the early days, I always envied people like saxophone players who had a close physical contact with the sound they produced, and later with guitarists. They could bend down on the strings and make it louder, whereas all I was doing was making an electrical connection and moving my foot down a fraction of an inch. It's a great paradox, therefore, that when synthesisers were developed, it brought a return to some kind of physical connection with the sound. There's so much control of notes in terms of bending notes, sliding notes, filters etc. I play all my solos on the synthesiser – I just don't get any feeling out of anything else now.

Already, he was convinced that synths would become the definitive keyboard instruments, as they seemed such a long-term advance in musical instrument making.

Much as Manfred loved keyboards, by mid-decade, he was learning to resist the all-too-easy temptation to swamp himself with them onstage. After the group had begun playing regularly in concert, he found that the instruments he was using were developing into a 'growing monster number', and soon realised that he could manage just as well with only three. As he told Chris Welch, the last thing he ever intended was to be 'surrounded' by them.

> Rushing from one to the other, you feel hemmed in, as if you were in prison. I don't feel the band is a vehicle for me to pose around the keyboards, and when the whole thing gets too heavy and noisy, I don't feel I can play any more. My whole instinct tells me to stop.

Manfred rarely played on sessions for other acts, but he was briefly invited to help Uriah Heep out in the studio on Moog. He was accordingly featured on two tracks, the ten-minute epic 'July Morning' and 'Tears in my Eyes', on their album *Look at Yourself*, recorded in July 1971 and released two months later. Characteristically modest about his contributions, he said he thought he played 'really badly, but they were happy'. It was a matter of keeping it within the family as both bands were among those managed by Gerry Bron, who had been looking after Manfred Mann since the mid-1960s. Gerry had suggested that Manfred should play on both tracks, even though their keyboard player Ken Hensley, who had never played synth before, rather resented having a guest musician being thrust on them.

When his present contract with Philips expired, Manfred would sign with Gerry's newly established Bronze Records, as Uriah Heep had recently done after issuing their first two albums on Vertigo. During its 15-year history, the small but select label roster also included Motörhead, Osibisa, Gene Pitney, Sally Oldfield, Manfred's old bandmate Tom McGuinness and his band McGuinness Flint, and singer-songwriter Tony Hazzard, who never had any success as a recording artist but had penned two of Manfred's 1960s hits, 'Ha! Ha! Said the Clown' and 'Fox on the Run', as well as Top 20 smashes for the likes of Herman's Hermits, The Tremeloes and Lulu.

All four members of the band went to Rome for a week to hone their act together, playing their debut there at the Piper Club in March. After further rehearsals, they were booked to headline an Australian tour in May, with Deep Purple supporting as Manfred Mann Chapter Three. However, as Chris Slade would subsequently point out, they were going on last, which wasn't quite the same thing as headlining. On one gig, about three-quarters of the way through the Deep Purple set, large sections of the audience were making their way out. They learnt that these people had to leave before the end to ensure they didn't miss the last bus or train home. Nobody had thought to cut the sets or alter the running time to start earlier.

During another show, while Colin was playing a solo on his bass, he broke a string. To his astonishment, a sharp-eyed roadie leapt up immediately and managed to replace it while he was still playing. Later he found out that the audience that night comprised some of the future members of AC/DC who could remember the occasion and remind him about it.

Colin's skills on the road were not confined to playing his instrument, even while one string was temporarily absent. He was also an expert with regard to the sound equipment, and on several of their overseas jaunts, the road crew would be waiting for him to arrive before setting everything up for the next gig. When they flew into an airport in Germany for one particular tour, the other three members went straight to the hotel while the crew took him directly to the first venue. They were puzzled as a radio station next door was transmitting through the amplifiers set up onstage and also seemed to be controlling Manfred's Minimoog. His solution was to send the crew out to obtain some tinfoil so they could wrap the amps and Manfred's keyboard with it. They then earthed the foil and Manfred played the whole show with a sheet over the keyboard. On another occasion, similar problems were solved only when Colin attached a cable from the earth point on the PA system to a metal pole in the tennis court outside.

The schedule in Australia was brought to a premature halt when it became apparent that the promoters, 'of dubious origin', were trying to pull a fast one on them. They played an additional gig at short notice and when their tour manager, David Joseph, went to collect payment, he was beaten up in a motel room in Melbourne, accused of embezzling money, thrown out and given 24 hours to leave the country. An armed mob turned up at the group's hotel looking for him, but he had prudently gone into hiding. Fearing for their safety, the group promptly cancelled all remaining dates and Manfred called a representative from the press, who escorted them to the airport and ensured they would be on the first plane back home. In Europe, a busy date sheet from mid-June onwards awaited them and they played several gigs in England and Wales, as well as festivals in Portugal, Switzerland, Sicily and Ireland in August and September.

Meanwhile, they had entered the studios to begin recording what would be their first single and then the debut album, both of which featured Manfred on his newly acquired synthesiser. Released in June as a 45, 'Living Without You' was a more commercial, uptempo arrangement of a ballad that Randy Newman had written and recorded on his eponymous album three years earlier. (The same record had also included his original version of 'So Long, Dad'.) When Manfred and Mick initially got together to assemble some kind of repertoire for rehearsals, they sat around a piano trying different numbers, and Mick later recalled that this was one of the first they ever attempted. Both were admirers of Randy Newman and it worked out so well that they simply had to record it themselves. They were very pleased with the completed result, though Manfred admitted to Gordon Coxhill of *NME* that he thought it was slightly out of character. 'When I do singles, my mind tends to work in a certain way. I seem to work in one kind of groove, or rut, if you like.' In any case, he'd started to look a little more kindly on their 1960s singles, about which he had been so dismissive at the time. 'I sit and play those old records now and I think maybe they weren't bad after all – quite good even.'

When it was issued in June 1971, credited to Manfred Mann, journalist Mark Plummer of *Melody Maker* told him he thought it sounded just like a hit. This left him with mixed feelings, fearing that it could return him to the 1960s situation with the band having to go back on the ballroom circuit and play to screaming 13-year-olds. It was 'fairly conventional', he conceded, but as he said, T. Rex and Deep Purple were also releasing successful singles and nobody would call them mainstream pop. A catchy, fairly upbeat song with a sunny acoustic guitar and synth intro that rather belied its doomy chorus of 'so hard living without you', it didn't chart in Britain despite generous airplay from Radio 1 that summer.

Despite this minor setback, Manfred was confident that the new line-up was the best and the most exciting with which he had ever played. He had been through the pop group stage, and then the arty stage, where they were deliberately playing uncommercial material in order to impress the serious critics how accomplished all of them were on their instruments. Now he simply wanted to go out and 'play good rock music so that it is an enjoyable evening for everyone', instead of needing to prove himself with songs featuring plenty of chords and clever changes in time signatures. 'But I'm not going to say that I am ashamed of making pop records any more.' A suitable balance had to be struck. It was important to keep things in perspective and not be obsessed about getting in the Top 30. Most people just hear the odd record on the radio,' he told Bob Edmands of *NME* a few years later. 'If they like it, they buy it. If they don't, they don't. It doesn't matter if a record fails. It's not a big disaster. Life carries on.'

A similar balance had to be maintained between going out to play live and also working in the studio, the latter being a necessary evil. 'Gigs are very important to me personally,' he said, 'but professionally, I'm more concerned about making good albums. I don't like making records but I need to spend much more time making them. I wish there were no such things as recording studios, but there are.'

To add to the new single and the B-side, 'Tribute', an instrumental by Manfred, the group completed seven more tracks intended for an album to be released on 3 September. Test pressings of *Stepping Sideways*, which comprised nine tracks, were made before the group had second thoughts and decided that it had something of a country rock flavour that they felt did not really become them. Once they began playing live, they found that four of the songs did not go down well onstage. These included 'Ned Kelly', 'It Ain't No Crime', the original take of 'Ashes to the Wind' that they would re-record for the second album, and their version of Neil Diamond's 'Holly Holy'. Release was therefore cancelled and additional material was recorded to replace them. The out-takes were shelved and would eventually appear in 2005 on a four-CD anthology, *Odds & Sods: Mis-takes & Out-takes*.

Undaunted by the failure of their debut, in September, the group issued a second single, 'Mrs Henry'. After the old band's version had remained in the vaults, it had also been offered to and covered by Chris Spedding (under its full title, 'Please Mrs Henry') on his 1970 debut album. Manfred Mann's version was a heavier, guitar-dominated rendition in which a powerful solo could not compensate for the lack of any commercial hook in what plainly wasn't one of Dylan's more interesting songs, and it went unnoticed by British and European radio programmers and buyers alike. A remix with some differences in the vocal and instrumental sections was issued as a single in America as 'Please Mrs Henry'. It peaked at number 112, a modest showing that would be bettered early the following year when 'Living Without You' reached No. 69.

A further name change was about to come, as they were discovering to their cost that reverting to the old 1960s moniker was not doing them any favours. The last thing the group and concert-goers had on their mind was a set that would cheerfully trot out the old pop smashes that they wanted to leave behind them. Chris later recalled that during the few weeks when they called themselves Manfred Mann again, they were finding it hard to get any work at all because by doing so, they were indelibly associating themselves with the 1960s and everybody, including the group themselves and the audience whose attention they were striving to capture, had moved on. 'So we became a so-called "underground band".'

'Mann' (almost) rhymed with 'Band', and he felt it would be appropriate to add another word in the middle to give some indication of the music they were playing. 'Arm band', 'elastic band', and 'head band' were all considered but rejected for various reasons. While they were waiting for their plane at Dublin airport after a concert in Ireland that October, Chris Slade suggested 'earth band'. As it suited their approval of the ecological movements then in progress and gaining support, they decided that was the one. 'The choice of name "Earth Band" is an effort to leave some of my past labelling behind,' Manfred told *Rolling Stone*. 'The problem has been that I have been stuck with a 1967 name and its past image that bears no relation to the music Earth Band are creating today. Also, I feel that is the best band I have ever had, and I think they should be out in front.'

Although much of Manfred's time was taken up with launching this new band, he still found time for other commitments. In October 1971, he began hosting a programme on BBC Radio 3, *Stereo Rock*, that was scheduled to run for three months. He also continued composing television jingles and music for commercials, including one for Nestlé's chocolate, recorded by the band.

Because a few forthcoming gigs were already booked and being advertised under the old name, they realised that any change would need to be phased in at a suitable time with sufficient notice. As from 1 December, they were officially Manfred Mann's Earth Band. They had already been using the name, as a small advertisement published in *Melody Maker* early in November would testify. At around the same time, additional tracks were recorded for the debut album, which they had decided would be named after the group. It was released in America on Polydor in January 1972 and in Britain on Philips a month later.

Left: *Manfred Mann's Earth Band.* The debut album by 'a band in search of a sound', 1972. *(Creature Music)*

Right: The band's British debut onstage, still billed as Manfred Mann, at Crystal Palace Bowl, London, with Desmond Dekker in June 1971.

Left: The group in 1972, with Manfred sporting a T-shirt bearing the new logo unveiled on their second album sleeve.

1972

Manfred Mann's Earth Band (1972)
Personnel:
Manfred Mann: Hammond organ, Minimoog synthesiser, backing vocals, lead vocals ('Part Time Man', 'I'm Up and I'm Leaving')
Mick Rogers: lead vocals, lead guitar
Colin Pattenden: bass guitar
Chris Slade: drums
Producers: Manfred Mann, Dave Hadfield, David Mackay
Studio: Maximum Sound, IBC, both London, summer and autumn 1971
Release date: US January 1972; UK February 1972
Chart placings: UK: – ; US: 138
Running time: 41:35
Label: Philips (UK), Polydor (US)
Side One: 1. California Coastline (Walt Meskell, Tim Martin) 2. Captain Bobby Stout (Lane Tietgen) 3. Sloth (Manfred Mann, Mick Rogers) 4. Living Without You (Randy Newman) 5. Tribute (Manfred Mann)
Side Two: 6. Please Mrs Henry (Bob Dylan) 7. Jump Sturdy (Dr John Creaux) 8. Prayer (Manfred Mann) 9. Part Time Man (David Sadler, Manfred Mann) 10. I'm Up and I'm Leaving (David Sadler, Manfred Mann)
Bonus tracks: Cohesion (1999)
11. Living Without You (single version, mono) 12. California Coastline (single version, mono) 13. Please Mrs Henry (single version, mono)

The group's debut album is hard to pigeonhole, or as some have perceptively said with hindsight, it is the work of 'a band in search of a sound'. Manfred himself had been through several changes in the previous few years. As the only member who was actively involved in production, this was in part, an experiment for him in combining jazz textures and the freedom he now had to break out of the three-minute straitjacket by embracing occasional fairly long keyboard and guitar solos and including a couple of prog-style instrumentals alongside commercially acceptable pop-rock. It suggests that he was torn between taking the music seriously enough, much of the time, while still allowing himself and the other three the odd left-field or semi-humorous diversion. The result is quite a varied mix of styles.

The opening track, 'California Coastline', was written by Walt Meskell and Tim Martin, best known for writing and producing for teen band

The DeFranco Family. A song about the delights of hitching around the American state in freezing weather, it sets the tone for much of their basic sound with some subtle Moog and Mick Rogers' muscular guitar, plus harmony chorus vocals. Apart from the percussion, the other instruments cut out part of the time to give some light and shade, and it is wrapped up with a few whooshing and whizzing noises towards the fade. For a brief period, it was under consideration as a third single, after 'Mrs Henry'.

At almost seven minutes in length, 'Captain Bobby Stout' benefits from gospelly vocals, insistent piano and stinging guitar work jostling with synths on the extended break. For a while, it was one of the high spots of their live show, with reviewers and fans alike finding the in-concert performances much more powerful than the studio version. The song was written by Californian performer Lane Tietgen, who had played with little-known bands such as The Serfs and The Jerry Hahn Brotherhood, but became better known after his songs were recorded by the Earth Band and others. Its subject, Captain Bobby Stout of the Wichita Police Department, was a well-known American lawman and member of the vice squad.

Their instrumental virtuosity continues with the shortest track of all, a 90-second instrumental 'Sloth', with its Hendrix-inspired guitar and delicate keyboard tinkling. It leads into the first single, 'Living Without You', where they transform Randy Newman's mournful ballad into a mid-tempo number enlivened particularly by the synth work, certainly the closest they came to pure pop-rock on the album. Whereas an earlier cover version on an album by Alan Price, which followed Randy's own recording hot on the heels of the original, was a faithful recreation of the composer's plaintive style, Manfred certainly make it more upbeat and commercial, although the lack of a really recognisable hook in the chorus makes one feel that as a song it is good as far as it goes but lacks that final spark.

'Tribute', an instrumental written by Manfred, is a five-minute ambient tune, reminiscent of Pink Floyd one moment and Santana the next. A slow, brooding bass riff and restrained beat on the drums provide a gentle backdrop for the keyboards and languid, Latin American-flavoured lead guitar, with the rhythm section cutting out about four minutes in and allowing a peaceful final minute or so that drifts gently into silence. It is basically a mood piece, a kind of theme, somewhat short of readily recognisable melody.

However, almost 30 years later, a sharp-eared German fan did recognise it, as a sample that Massive Attack had used on 'Black Milk', a track on their album *Mezzanine* in 1998. The Bristol trip hop collective had sampled 120 bars out of 128 from the original track, retaining an identical drum pattern, hi-hat and bassline. When Manfred was tipped off by the fan, he sued for plagiarism, claiming damages of £100,000 from Massive Attack and seeking an injunction to stop sales of the album. Both parties subsequently settled the case amicably out of court.

The second single, 'Mrs Henry', is certainly a less radio-friendly proposition than the first was. Chugging bass and drums allow Mick a chance to shine on vocal and guitar, but again there is no discernible hook to give it that edge over anything else on the radio at the same time. About two and a half minutes in, the vocals on the heavily repeated chorus crossfade into a guitar-led jam that hovers round one chord for the next one and a half minutes or so before revisiting the chorus that continues until the fade. As a foray into blues-based rock veering part of the way towards heavy metal, it ticks the right boxes, but cries out for further development instead of being stuck in the same groove for much of the time. Anything but a 'potential hit 45', in fact.

A Dr John song, 'Jump Sturdy', adds a New Orleans vibe to the flavour. Jump Sturdy, according to the lyrics, was a woman who 'came out the swamps like a crazy fool ... a treacherous lady, she never met much harm'. Mainly guitar-based, with a funky beat from the drums and some jazzy runs on the piano during the final minute, it marks another direction for the quartet.

'Prayer', the second of Manfred's own compositions, brings a quasi-religious lyric – 'Tell me Lord, don't you really see, The way I am and the things I could be?' – with a tune driven by a bass riff that sits on one chord for almost the first five minutes. Synth adds some colour, and about halfway through it turns into a jam with heavy guitar riffing and vigorous pounding on the drums, after which the vocals return. In the last 40 seconds, it shifts key as guitar and keyboards play in unison until bass and drums bring them to a tidy finish. Some fans have seen it as being based largely on 'Dealer Dealer' from *As Is*, the album the old group released in 1966 as their debut with Michael d'Abo on vocals. To these ears, however, there is only a passing similarity, in the insistent riff that powers both songs. Lyrically they have nothing in common, the older song being the plaintive lament of an unlucky gambler.

Two songs co-written by Manfred with friend David Sadler, both featuring Manfred on lead vocal for a change, conclude the album. 'Part Time Man' is the sardonic, somewhat futurist tale of a veteran who has just returned home from fighting in World War Three, answers a job vacancy in the paper looking for a part-time man, goes to the factory where he waits in a queue, fills in a lengthy questionnaire but is rewarded by a shake of the head. Summarised in cold print like that may not exactly illustrate the humour well, but taken as a whole, it's a rather clever portrayal of the drudgery and soullessness that's the lot of jobseekers the world over. Slow and restrained, backed largely by piano and guitars, mostly acoustic and kept well in the background, there are touches of a recorder-like sound from the synths, and Mick sweetening the sound with harmonies on the chorus. Manfred's world-weary voice here sounds remarkably like Randy Newman, whose own style must have been an influence.

'I'm Up and I'm Leaving' is in a similar vein. A solo ballad from Manfred with guitar and rhythm section noticeably absent, he sings in a higher register than usual about going to the great city and getting on the Green Line bus so he can join the rat race. Double-tracked vocals, gentle piano and keyboard touches sounding like an accordion add a mournful air. As the first two singles had enjoyed minor American success, these last two songs, strangely untypical of the group's usual style and hardly commercial, sounding more like a solo singer-songwriter, followed on both sides of a 45 in July and similarly made the Top 200. They had a feel slightly reminiscent of The Band, and it would have been hard to find a British combo at the start of the 1970s who did not admit to being a huge fan of the Canadian-American group and freely acknowledged them as an influence on their music.

As for the four tracks that were rejected, in three of them, there is more of a country rock feel as well as a marked lack of synthesiser and keyboard sounds, with piano underpinning the rhythm section but taking something of a secondary role, in marked contrast to the main flavour of the group's work. 'Ned Kelly' is a song about the 19th-century Australian outlaw, written by Trevor Lucas, an Australian singer-songwriter who was briefly a member of Fairport Convention, and the short-lived Fotheringay, both with his wife, Sandy Denny. The latter band recorded it on their first (and last) album in 1970 as 'The Ballad of Ned Kelly (Poor Ned)'. One year later, the Earth Band turn it into a jaunty, jug-band-flavoured folk-rock singalong with a few touches of banjo and slide guitar, not to mention some George Harrisonesque lead guitar.

'Ashes to the Wind', a song they evidently felt they could improve on and therefore revisited on the second album, consists of a slow verse and a faster call-and-respond chant section, a pattern they repeat during the four and a half minutes. At times it sounds close to Jethro Tull with its use of acoustic guitar and flute, or possibly flute-like sounds produced on the keyboard, and a touch of guitar played through a Leslie speaker.

'Ain't No Crime' sounds more like The Lovin' Spoonful in 'Daydream' mode, or The Kinks' music-hall style. Another jaunty singalong number with everyone joining in the chorus, there are some neat touches of mildly jazz-flavoured acoustic and electric guitar filling the gaps, until the final minute, which is dominated mainly by a break on the synth. It would not have sounded out of place as a B-side of one of the late 1960s singles during the d'Abo era.

Finally, 'Holly Holy' started life as a Top 10 hit for Neil Diamond in America in 1969, at a time when he was little-known in Britain except as a writer of songs that were successful for The Monkees and Lulu. Neil's slow gospel treatment, complete with choir and almost five minutes long, is given more of a folk-rock atmosphere by the Earth Band. They take it at a much brisker pace than its writer's version, with Mick's voice pitched noticeably higher. Close to folk-rock territory, it's powered from the start by acoustic guitar chords, piano and subtle synth phrases, joined by an insistent bass riff and slide guitar, along with a tambourine enhancing the drums. Although they omit the bridge verse, they pull a clever trick by taking the second verse up one key, then about 30 seconds later dropping down to the original key again. Most of the last minute is taken up with an instrumental break until the fade, with guitar and synth playing complementary lines. As the entire tune sits atop two chords – make that four if you count the key change – there remains the feeling that they could have done something a little more ambitious with it towards the end. That minor criticism apart, it is a good commercial result with a song that could have easily been a contender for a hit single in Britain, especially as the writer's original never repeated its American success across the Atlantic.

Reaction to the album on release was largely indifferent in Britain, but critics in America gave it an enthusiastic welcome. In *High Fidelity*, Henry Edwards said that they'd proved themselves greatly superior to other acts in the British Blues Invasion of the 1970s by 'displaying a dedication to the music rather than flaunting their individual abilities'. At the end of the decade, Robert Christgau would place it at No. 17 in his list of the best albums of the last ten years, calling it 'an extraordinary cult record' that achieved 'art-commerce' synthesis. *AllMusic Guide* was no less enthusiastic. According to J.P. Ollio, it was 'a completely

satisfying album and one of the most underrated of the 1970s', in
which the Earth Band explored 'arty and progressive directions' without
succumbing to the weight of their own pretensions. Reviewing a reissue
after Bronze Records had acquired the rights to the group's first three
albums originally released in Britain by Phonogram (the first two on the
Philips label and the third on Vertigo) in 1978, Hugh Fielder of *Sounds*
was less won over as he commented that the record 'doesn't really hang
together and it's clear that the group were still settling in'. 'Please Mrs
Henry', he opined, was given a ponderous, chanting treatment that
sounded more like The Edgar Broughton Band than Manfred Mann.
He did, however, praise Manfred for 'demonstrating his skill in finding
songs to suit his own purpose'. In a retrospective round-up nearly 30
years later, Tim Jones in *Record Collector* summed up the overall feel
as that 'of a bright and breezy soft rocking album, with hints of hippie
vocals and Harvey Mandel-style period guitar'.

Every Manfred Mann's Earth Band album would include at least one
or two cover versions, alongside songs and instrumentals written by
Manfred himself, some in collaboration with one or more of the other
members, others with outside co-writers. It had also been noticed that
all of the old group's hits in the 1960s from 'Do Wah Diddy Diddy'
onwards had similarly been the work of different songsmiths, although
the B-sides and some of the album tracks were their own work.

When asked some years later by online interviewer Gary James about
the generally small proportion of original music they ever recorded, he
replied that while some of the band members were good writers, he
personally never felt their material would be able to compete with the
really good ones like The Beatles or The Rolling Stones who had raised
the bar so high. He could not do better than them, he realised, but to
him, it was not a problem. Neither Frank Sinatra nor the jazz musicians
he enjoyed when he was growing up were songwriters or composers, as
well as singers or players as well. 'I never thought that was essential. It
wasn't part of my background. I didn't see why you had to be a writer
to be a performer. Certainly, when an orchestra plays Beethoven you
don't complain they didn't write their own symphony.'

To Merrill Shindler of *Rolling Stone*, he said he always saw his
strengths as more in the field of musicianship and arrangement. 'I judge
myself to be a better interpreter, a better arranger than a songwriter.'
There had been a prevailing view in the 1960s that, in Britain at least,
the groups who relied on outside writers for their A-sides were generally

the ones whose success tailed off sharply by mid-decade and soon found themselves relegated to the nostalgia package nights circuit where they could always earn a lucrative trade playing their old hits, but rarely if ever troubled the Top 50 again. Manfred Mann's Earth Band were almost unique in bucking the trend and relying to a large extent on cover versions. In their case, the main difference was that they went to enormous lengths to refashion and rearrange the songs, usually ending up with a result radically different from the original.

As for the material they wrote themselves, a large proportion was instrumental and grew out of group improvisations. The vocal numbers generally eschewed the common pop-rock themes of love and lust, and, apart from environmental themes (appropriately for an act with a name like theirs), avoided political messages. 'With God on Our Side', which had attracted so much attention and airplay as an EP track with the old band in 1965, had been an almost uniquely controversial item in the back catalogue. Manfred maintained that music was much more important 'and delivers a far more fundamental, subconscious, emotional thing than all the verbalising in the world. A lot of people usually feel they have to verbalise a big message (that) the band's trying to convey.'

The Earth Band played about a dozen gigs in England over the first three months of 1972, followed by one in Belfast in April, and then toured Australia from May to July. Returning to play in the latter was important for them as it gave them the confidence in themselves, showing them that they really were good enough. 'We hadn't reached anywhere near what we wanted to do,' he said, 'and I thought we came off very well.'

While not on the road, they were in the studio, recording a second album, *Glorified Magnified*. By this time, they had begun to develop their own distinctive style, with Manfred and Mick jamming onstage while Colin and Chris kept the rhythm section going, in order to provide longer instrumental sections. After seeing them in concert, some reviewers would comment that a noticeable feature of their music was the way Mick and Manfred played so closely together, with the guitarist producing a riff, the keyboard player following it and most of the instrumental passages being thus based around the guitar and organ or Moog inter-soloing. As albums with their built-in constraints of around 20 minutes per side strictly limited any opportunity to present their interactive side on vinyl (or cassette), and as marathon tracks taking up around one side smacked of severe self-indulgence, it was no wonder that they much preferred playing live to working in the studio.

Mick also recognised that all four of them made a perfect combination, with the bassist and drummer helping to make the group something special, and without hogging the spotlight. It was their 'pure energy,' he said, 'really tight, like the early Free rhythm section but looser, and this enabled Manfred and myself to have a lot of freedom on top of that, and it used to fly.' Chris also fondly remembered his stint with the group as 'a very creative time because I was songwriting, co-producing, trying experimental ideas, jamming onstage, flying off on musical tangents, very rewarding.'

Airplay in Britain for their records was limited at first as they were seen as very much an albums band at a time when there was still something of a gulf, albeit a narrowing one, between singles and albums artists. They did, however, record several sessions for BBC Radio 1 during their first three years. The first was in July 1971 for Dave Lee Travis's more mainstream pop daytime programme, while four subsequent ones were taped over the next 18 months for *Top Gear*, the evening progressive rock showcase presented in turns by John Peel, Tommy Vance and Pete Drummond. Some of the tapes have since been lost, although logs show that the missing items included 'Meat', 'Ashes in the Wind' and 'One Way Glass', all of which would appear on the next album, 'Dealer', presumably the old 'As Is' number, and 'Messin'', destined to be the title track of album number three. The surviving items were released some years later as the fourth and final part of the *Manfred Mann: Radio Days* series on CD and vinyl. They included 'Happy Being Me', which remained a favourite from the Chapter Three era, 'Captain Bobby Stout', 'Get Your Rocks Off', the evergreen 'Mighty Quinn', and the intriguingly named 'Bubblegum and Kipling', an earlier version of what would become 'Earth the Circle, Part 2' on the fourth album. The original title had been inspired by the name of a book of short stories by American author Tom W. Mayer.

As a live unit onstage, they were confident that they were improving all the time, especially if reviews were anything to go by, and for Manfred, it had rapidly become by far the best of the groups with which he had been involved. In the studio, they also developed a technique of crossfading instruments in the mix, which generally comprised fading out the drums and bringing in keyboards at strategic points, especially on the longer tracks, often taking the drums in again later for a powerful end. This was all reflected in the new album, released in September. Other musicians were also exploring the principle for similar effect, notably Mike Oldfield, who was about to begin recording *Tubular Bells*, released the following year.

Glorified Magnified (1972)

Personnel:

Manfred Mann: organ, Minimoog synthesiser, vocals

Mick Rogers: guitar, vocals

Colin Pattenden: bass guitar

Chris Slade: drums

Producers: Manfred Mann, Dave Hadfield, Tom McGuinness (track 9)

Studio: Maximum Sound, London, 1972

Release date: September 1972

Chart placings: UK: – , US: –

Running time: 41:35

Label: Philips (UK), Polydor (US)

Side One: 1. Meat (Manfred Mann) 2. Look Around (Chris Slade) 3. One Way Glass (Manfred Mann, Peter Thomas) 4. I'm Gonna Have You All (Manfred Mann)

Side Two: 5. Down Home (Mick Rogers) 6. Our Friend George (Manfred Mann) 7. Ashes to the Wind (Charyl Edmonds, Jonah Thompson) 8. Wind (Manfred Mann, Mick Rogers, Colin Pattenden, Chris Slade) 9. It's All Over Now, Baby Blue (Bob Dylan) 10. Glorified Magnified (Manfred Mann)

Bonus tracks: Cohesion (1999)

11. Meat (single version) (Manfred Mann) 12. It's All Over Now, Baby Blue (single version) (Bob Dylan)

The second album was the work of a group that were beginning to explore and develop the possibilities open to them after spending a year or so on the road. Now they were gelling onstage as opposed to getting used to each other as musicians, experimenting within the confines of the studio at Maximum Sound, and clearly revelling in it. If the debut had been recorded under pressure by a quartet whose members were torn between keeping one foot in the radio-friendly pop-rock market by recording potential singles for an audience that also loved The Rolling Stones and Led Zeppelin, and putting a toe in the water with more spacey, left-field fare in Pink Floyd or Hawkwind vein, the second one finds them nailing their colours more clearly to the 'heavy meets prog rock' genre. Anything less might have been seen as a hesitant reversal towards the 1960s sound and, therefore, the image that they were anxious to leave far behind them.

Viewed several decades on, some fans regard this as not so much a progressive rock album – only one track exceeds five minutes, with no long-drawn-out epics in sight – as more hard rock, with Manfred's keyboard work a little less prominent than usual and Mick's guitar to the fore. Ironically, it also finds Manfred much more dominant as a writer, with four numbers entirely his own work and two more featuring him as a collaborator. Some see it as a transitional record, as if the quartet were unsure whether to embrace a pop-rock style with occasional forays into hard and heavy material, or label themselves as a full-tilt prog outfit.

The opening track and first single is one of the most bizarre they ever recorded, certainly in their early days. 'Meat' was intended as a gentle satire on Chris's vegetarian lifestyle, a relic from an age when non-carnivores were more in the minority. It's almost a comic number, set to a jazzy 'Resurrection Shuffle' rhythm on the drums, with the phrases 'don't eat meat', and 'jump down, turn around' sung regularly over the top. One can almost imagine it being played as a light-hearted dance tune at discos, which was anything but the target audience the group were looking for. Maybe it was aiming at a Frank Zappa kind of quirkiness. Fun, perhaps, but a great piece of music, rather less so.

'Look Around' suggests that the group were chasing a blues-rock direction at least part of the time. Shades of Alvin Lee and Ten Years After come on this song, dominated by Mick's vocals and guitar, with Manfred's keyboards shining through fitfully. Colin provides an insistent bass riff, while for most of the time, it hovers on one chord. After a fairly long guitar solo and a flurry on the drums, it changes pitch, the vocals return and a more dramatic, slower coda finishes proceedings.

The slow 'One Way Glass' offers a total contrast. In just two verses, the melancholy lyrics sung by Mick declaim the desolation of a loner begging for a window with one way glass, where he can 'look out on the world and watch people pass' without being seen himself. Lead guitar curls around the lines, and it ends with a brief passage on Moog, sounding rather like a bagpipe lament. The song had originally appeared on the first Manfred Mann Chapter Three album three years earlier, a very different, rather more spirited version with lead vocal by Manfred, who co-wrote it, with a prominent horn section on the break. It was also the A-side of a single by The John Schroeder Orchestra, 'Featuring Chris – Vocals', released in November 1971. This was Chris Thompson, who, by coincidence, would become a member of the band five years later.

A stomping, northern soul-like beat is the order for 'I'm Gonna Have You All'. Mick unleashes an impassioned solo on guitar, while towards the end, Manfred's Moog plays minor variations, never straying very far from one note. This upbeat mood continues on the first track on side two, 'Down Home', a jaunty mid-paced number with a commercial hook, lyrics about how good it will be to get away back to where he belongs, out of 'bad luck and trouble'. Musically it hits a southern boogie feel, similar in mood to Little Feat. Mick delivers probably his best guitar work on the whole album, while Manfred adds some comic flourishes, even one or two out of tune notes on the piano (to say nothing of somebody snorting, if you listen carefully) and a change in key near the end gives it an additional lift.

'Our Friend George' unleashes some real vitriol and attacking musicianship to match. Whether George was a real person or a fictional character concerns us not, but he is clearly no friend – 'something just ain't true about you' runs one typical line. The tempo brings blues, funk and hard rock together in equal measure, with a good example of the crossfade technique where drums almost disappear to allow the guitar to surge forth, bringing the whole song to a fierce crescendo with everything hitting full volume.

Ringing the changes again, 'Ashes to the Wind' by contrast is an almost folksy ballad. Re-recorded and at just over two minutes, less than half the length of the earlier version, it opens on a dreamy vocal, similar to some of Traffic's semi-acoustic pieces and wistful acoustic guitar. Synths, which can barely be heard on the original version, lead guitar and bass add some contrast to make the song portentously doomy one moment, ethereal the next, with an elegant lead break and a few seconds of a cappella to finish. It is followed by 'Wind', an instrumental that develops from a simple bass guitar (following the same two-note figure throughout) and drum pattern to some intriguingly harsh synth effects and a sudden ending.

If it's Manfred Mann, then there can't be a Dylan song very far away. 'It's All Over Now, Baby Blue', a number said to have been written by him early in 1965 as a kind of farewell to the young folk performer and a move away from his protest singer era, follows the mood of the original. After the predominantly acoustic backing for the first two verses, supplemented with some fine growling bass runs and restrained lead guitar, a more chunky electric rhythm guitar joins in while the drums gradually let rip – with keyboards very little in evidence. A three-minute edit, fading about a minute before the full album version does, appeared as an American single.

Finally, the album track hints – in title as well as in style – at the progressive rock experiments that would go on to characterise the next few albums. 'Glorified Magnified' itself is another instrumental, with sometimes discordant but intriguing synth doodles over the opening drum pattern. Organ and lead guitar pile on the attack, there are some sudden time signature changes, and during the last minute or so, a choir join in, singing the title phrase over the instruments. It all ends on a peaceful movement with the heavenly voices and a single organ note. As a footnote, the front sleeve design marked the first appearance of the group's iconic red, blue and black logo.

Chris was now beginning to make his contributions to the writing as well as playing drums, though 'Look Around' was a rarity in that he was given the sole credit. It always amused him when people saw the name Slade on their albums and, not believing that a drummer could be such an accomplished lyricist as well, immediately thought that Noddy Holder must have been involved.

Apart from one track, the album was produced by Manfred and Dave Hadfield. The exception was 'It's All Over Now, Baby Blue', with Manfred's guitarist from the previous decade, Tom McGuinness, sharing the producer's chair. Their paths had crossed both ways that year, for the latter's group, McGuinness Flint, had made two very successful singles and two albums as the new decade dawned. They then broke up when Benny Gallagher and Graham Lyle, who had written most of the songs, disliked playing live and left to work together as a duo. Recruiting Dixie Dean on bass, they renamed themselves Coulson, Dean, McGuinness and Flint for another album, *Lo and Behold*, featuring their versions of ten little-known Bob Dylan songs he had never issued himself, some from his early days and others from the basement tapes sessions. Manfred nominally joined them as co-producer on the record and played organ on one track from the sessions, 'Tiny Montgomery', although according to Tom, he was not present for much of the time. While not a commercial success, the album was highly regarded by critics at the time, and ever since. *Rolling Stone* called it 'the best Dylan album since *Blonde on Blonde*', and like the early Earth Band albums, it has long since been regarded as something of an overlooked classic despite disappointing sales and a failure to make the charts.

The idea of gaining a first refusal on some of the songwriter's lesser-known numbers had always appealed to Manfred and his former fellow band member ever since they had taken 'If You Gotta Go, Go Now' into the top three in 1965. 'We were very reluctant to bring out Dylan material that was on a Dylan album,' he told Joe Klee of *Rock Magazine*. 'Generally speaking, once everybody knew the Dylan version, I was much more reluctant to pick up on it. We seemed to be lucky enough to get hold of tapes that hadn't been released.'

At this point, Manfred's track record in recording little-known songs by Mr Zimmerman, or alternatively getting more-or-less exclusive access to demo versions of his work long before they entered the public consciousness, was second to none in Britain. Therefore it did show a lack of imagination in recording a satisfactory if hardly trailblazing, version of 'It's All Over Now, Baby Blue', which was already well known through his own version on *Bringing It All Back Home* in 1965, as well as those by Joan Baez (a No. 22 British hit later that year) and Them, featuring Van Morrison. Earth Band talents might have been deployed better in seeking out one of the many just as worthy Dylan obscurities that would have benefited in being brought to more general notice. In spite of this, the song remained Mick Rogers' favourite of all their Dylan covers.

Another album released that year in Britain reunited the former colleagues, with Manfred playing organ and Tom guitar – Mike Hugg's solo work *Somewhere*. Additional session musicians on the latter included Mick Rogers on guitar and former Herd, future Status Quo keyboard player Andy Bown on bass, while Dave Hadfield was the producer.

Around the same time, a soundtrack for the soft-porn film *Swedish Fly Girls* (a Danish picture, despite the title) was released only in America on the Juno label. Most of the music was written by Mose Henry and lyrics by director Jack O'Connell, and produced by Manfred Mann. Four tracks were credited to Sandy Denny, another to Melanie (Safka), and the remaining 11 – including a different version of Manfred Mann Chapter Three's song, 'Broken-Glass Lives' – to nobody in particular. The record is extremely rare, regarded as only of curiosity value, and is said by the few people who admit to having heard it to be less than mildly captivating.

With no hit singles to their name, *Top of the Pops* was still off their radar, although it would not be for much longer. They had, however, been given a spot on an early series of *The Old Grey Whistle Test*, at that time the BBC's only other regular music television programme, a late-night weekly show focusing on album-oriented artists. In April 1972, they were featured playing 'Meat' and 'Our Friend George', from the album that was still in progress.

Glorified Magnified received a better reaction in Britain than its predecessor and sold respectably, although without charting. There was still some confusion about the group's name, and in November, 'Meat' was issued as a single, credited to Earth Band. Radio interest was lacking, maybe in part because not everybody had yet made the connection with Manfred. In retrospect, it may have been just as well that the single never went on the Radio 1 daytime playlist or troubled the Top 50. For it to have done otherwise might have saddled them with an unwanted and undeserved reputation for releasing novelty records that, once acquired, would be hard to shake off. In America, Polydor issued 'It's All Over Now, Baby Blue' instead as a 45, although again without success. The song had never been a hit over there, not even the version by Joan Baez that had scored in Britain.

It was on the other side of the Atlantic – where the name of Manfred Mann had been of only fleeting interest in the 1960s, so they did not have the baggage of their pop hits – that interest in the band seemed stronger. After further dates in Britain for about three months from August 1972 onwards, at the end of November, they began a stateside tour, making their debut there at the Whisky a Go Go, Los Angeles, then gigs at the New York Academy of Music, sharing the bill with Uriah Heep, and at the University of Miami. One show at the latter towards the end of December was cut short by Miami police, and concluded with a riot by students at the University lasting a couple of hours. Local residents had complained about the volume, the power was turned off during the encore, and the band members had to hide in a dressing room until the hubbub had died down.

Despite such misadventures that were very much an occupational hazard, Manfred always loved playing live. When asked by interviewers what he enjoyed most about it, he always found it difficult to explain. One thing he was sure of was that, for him, music at a concert was always about the rhythm and the groove. It was something he had assimilated from his love of and growing up with American music. Europe, he once said – well aware that a lot of people would not thank him for saying so – was 'a groove-free zone'. European musicians, he insisted, simply didn't understand it the way that American players did. Modern technology wasn't the answer to everything. It might allow somebody to dial up groove or a rhythm pattern on a machine, but because the Europeans did not recognise it, he said, 'They often just choose the wrong item out of the 278 million choices on a modern computer.' Software could perform many tasks, he acknowledged, and assist the human brain but never replace it.

Since learning the piano, he had always been in awe of American musicians. From the great jazz players of the 1950s, to the largely unsung heroes who contributed to sessions on the Motown and Stax soul records of the golden era throughout the 1960s, they were the source of the work he always admired most. Some great music had come from Britain, where players might be more imaginative and experimental, but on the other side of the Atlantic, groove was in the blood.

Above all, he was relishing the new musical freedom that was becoming a characteristic of the 1970s. A few years later, he admitted there was simply no comparison between this one and the 1960s, when there was 'this continual voice telling you that you weren't doing what you should be doing. That you sold out to yourself.' He was wary of making such statements to the music press as he felt there was nothing worse than reading about someone who disowned a musical past that a lot of people knew him for. There was nobody else to blame; 'no-one with a gun at my head making me do it'. But he had still been more than happy to break out of the 1960s pop straitjacket.

Journalists on both sides of the Atlantic had readily appreciated the new group's strengths. Joe Klee was impressed with Manfred's synthesiser playing and the three newer musicians behind him.

Mick Rogers has an easy style that fits well with Manfred's low-pressure concepts. This group is not out to blast anybody's eardrums and the vocals are sufficiently non-distorted that you can actually understand the words Mick is singing. Colin Pattenden plays bass expertly but mostly keeps out of the spotlight. So, in fact, does drummer Chris Slade. By comparison with so many superstar drummers, it is his very lack of egocentric spotlight-hogging that causes much notice of this shy Welshman.

Similar praise came from another writer, Jim Bickhart, who opined after a show at the Whisky a Go Go that when Manfred's synthesiser work reached its most unearthly heights:

The band's progressive funk was quite effective. The worst moments were only mildly boring, and one could always amuse oneself watching Manfred conduct the band, play his organ and synthesiser and do a shuffling dance all at one up behind the organ.

While the singles and albums had only fared modestly in the charts so far, it was apparent that with further exposure and live work, success on a wider scale would surely be just a matter of time.

Right: *Glorified Magnified.* The second album, marked a shift into heavy rock. The US sleeve showed the logo on a black background, 1972. *(Creature Music)*

Glorified Magnified

Above: *Messin'.* The sleeve shows a gas mask in front of a desert landscape, with planet earth visible through the filter, 1973. *(Creature Music)*

Right: 'Get Your Rocks Off', one of their several Bob Dylan cover versions, released as a single, in April 1973.

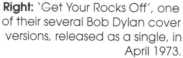

1973

A packed working schedule during the new year saw Manfred Mann's Earth Band rarely off the road or out of the studio. From January to early April, they were playing gigs in England. Even though they had yet to put in an appearance in the Top 20, as a live act, their reputation was constantly growing. After a concert at London City University in January, Jeff Ward noted in *Melody Maker* that they were 'an exacting group of musicians who, greatly to their credit, fully understand the evasive qualities of volume and how it can be intelligently used to the best effect, and for real impact'. While they were onstage, 'it was hardly possible to fault the sound, it was easy on the ear, clear and clean, yet the centre of a high energy power zone, that could whip up excitement, even in a hall like this one that lacked atmosphere and proper lighting.' As for the interplay between them, 'Manfred has a mastery over his keyboard console. He knows what to leave out as well as what to put in, and the others in the band follow his lead. They're unfussy, selective and let their versatility bring out only their best.'

During the rest of April, they played Europe, including festivals at Dortmund and Mannheim in Germany one week apart, sharing a bill with Atomic Rooster, Jackson Heights, Soft Machine and Emerson, Lake & Palmer at the first, with Hawkwind, Spirit, Brian Auger's Oblivion Express and UFO at the second. In May and June, they toured the United States and Canada with various acts, including ELO, Savoy Brown, Status Quo and ZZ Top. Some of these groups looked like an odd pairing on paper, but as Francis Rossi of Quo later noted in his memoirs, in those days, promoters didn't place much emphasis on putting together bills that would suit just one particular audience. It was more about working hard each night with the aim of winning over music fans 'wherever you happened to have arrived on the map'.

They had no difficulty in selling out concerts wherever they played and always met with an enthusiastic reception, although not all American critics were ready to give them an unqualified thumbs-up. One anonymous reviewer, writing in *The Village Voice* after a show at the Academy of Music, New York, in June, said that 'on stage, they tend to let their ideas run away with themselves and once guitarist Mick Rogers starts swapping phrases with Manfred's synthesiser, things get dull rather quickly, even on their best songs. This latest chapter of Manfred's ten-year search for the perfect, unobtainable music is generally more successful on their records.'

During the second half of the year, they devoted their energies to shows in England, Germany and Sweden. In the summer, they also released a third album which saw an in-house move from the Philips label to the company's progressive outlet Vertigo. A few weeks later, after four years of trying, Manfred enjoyed that elusive major hit single in Britain. The fourth album would follow before the year was out.

Messin' (1973)

Personnel:
Manfred Mann: organ, Minimoog synthesiser, vocals
Mick Rogers: guitar, vocals
Colin Pattenden: bass guitar
Chris Slade: drums
Additional musicians:
Laurie Baker: machines and zoo (Messin')
Lisa Strike, Vicki Brown, Judith Powell, Ruby James: backing vocals
Producer: Manfred Mann
Studio: Maximum Sound, London, 1972
Release date: June 1973
Chart placings: UK: – , US: 196
Running time: 41:16
Label: Vertigo (UK), Polydor (US)
Side One: 1. Messin' (Mike Hugg) 2. Buddah (Manfred Mann, Mick Rogers) 3. Cloudy Eyes (Manfred Mann)
Side Two: 4. Get Your Rocks Off (Bob Dylan) 5. Sadjoy (Manfred Mann) 6. Black and Blue (Matt Taylor, Phil Manning) 7. Mardi Gras Day (Dr John Creaux)
Bonus tracks: Cohesion (1998)
8. Pretty Good (John Prine) 9. Cloudy Eyes (single edit) (Manfred Mann)

The album was issued in America as *Get Your Rocks Off*, after the American single, with a different sleeve design and a minor alteration in the track listing. 'Black and Blue', with its theme of slavery – although by no means supporting the principle – was thought too controversial and replaced by 'Pretty Good', which was included some years later as a bonus track on the British and European releases.

Songs protesting about the state of the planet and voicing environmental concerns were few and far between at the start of the 1970s, so hats off to Manfred and the team for being among the pioneers. Joining Joni Mitchell's 'Big Yellow Taxi' ('They paved paradise and put up a parking lot'), Lindisfarne's 'All Fall Down' ('Who needs the trees and the flowers to grow?'), and even The Osmonds' 'Crazy Horses' ('Crazy horses, smoking up the sky'), to single out three of the best known, was a song written by Mike Hugg and recorded on the third, unreleased Chapter Three album in 1971, as well as for a BBC Radio 1 session the following year. Had it been condensed into a shorter, more radio-friendly affair and issued as a 45, it might have become better known. However, a long-drawn-out ten-minute cut never stood much chance of reaching an audience beyond the group's most devoted fans. Originally called 'Messin' Up the Land', it makes a serious point with its message to people who live up in their castle in the sky and can easily forget about the problems of an earth 'going down in pollution blues' – 'you still breathe in the same air as me, eating, drinking, poisoning where it should be'.

Musically it was a little like grunge before its time (like the lyrical concerns, perhaps). The Chapter Three version, almost nine minutes in length, appeared on *Odds & Sods: Mis-takes and Out-takes* over 30 years later, with Mike Hugg's vocal set over a mid-tempo track reminiscent in mood to The Temptations' 'Ball of Confusion', incorporating an extended, semi-improvisatory passage from the horns. The Earth Band slow the tempo down, with echoes of a not dissimilar epic, 'Feel too Good', from the third Move album 'Looking On', or the dense swamp-like guitar-driven sound of Creedence Clearwater Revival's 'Run Through the Jungle' into an orgy of metallic riffs delivered on Mick Rogers' six-string, supplemented by Manfred's flights of fancy on the Moog. An overture of sorts is provided by a wash of machines and zoo sonic effects, which surfaces later on in the track, while the backing vocal quartet chant the 'we're messin' up the earth, we're messin' up the sea, we're messin' up the air, messin' up on you and me' after the verses.

Reviewing the album in *Rolling Stone*, Stephen Holden saw it as a very short blues fragment repeated over and over again 'until it accumulates the force of a tribal chant intended to exorcise the demons of ecological catastrophe'. After about four minutes, there is a brief lull, before Mick lets loose on guitar, supported ably by Manfred and the rhythm section, with particularly impressive bass runs from Colin. A reprise of the chorus comes shortly before the end, or rather takes it to a brief coda of chattering monkeys in the jungle. All in all, it delivers a powerful statement. It's an oddly likeable confection that may sound incomprehensibly weighty on the first listen, before it all falls into place. While the thought lingers that a little judicious tape editing could have delivered an improved, more concise helping (and more importantly, one that radio programmers would have found more acceptable), the power of the full track shines through on closer acquaintance.

Should anybody have missed the point, the message is driven home by the original gatefold sleeve design. A giant gas mask in front of a bright blue sky and desert landscape has a hole where the filter should be, and through it can be seen an image of planet earth. In his review of the album for *Melody Maker*, Chris Welch described it as 'a vision of the earth as a parched desert, witnessed by an astronaut from outer space at some point in the near future'.

A ten-minute magnum opus is followed by a seven-minute one. 'Buddah' basically consists of two sections. The first is a three-minute vocal part, in which Mick sings of meeting Buddah in the street, then coming face to face with Jesus in a riot zone, and finally, Moses in a Cadillac. It's possibly a satire on religion – let the listener decide – set to a slow tempo with tasteful lead guitar picking, which make you wonder whether Boston were inspired to write 'More Than a Feeling' after hearing it. After that comes a heavy tattoo spearheaded by guitar and drums, which serves partly to obscure what sounds like a fast forward of the entire lyrical section, followed by a faster, battle-like instrumental break on guitar and keyboards like Deep Purple venturing into jazz. A stately passage, later on, threatens to break into a thunderous drum solo at the end. If anyone still thought that Manfred Mann's Earth Band were in the least pop, this alone would have served to dispel any such notions.

Written by Manfred for a musical that never came to fruition, the instrumental 'Cloudy Eyes' sounds not unsurprisingly like a foray into film soundtrack territory. A tasteful, slow guitar-led piece sounds like Santana one moment and Elton John's 'Funeral for a Friend' the next, although without any variation in tempo. About four minutes in, it fades, only to return seconds later, fading in softly and finishing about a minute later as a wistful drone for guitar and keyboards.

If you were wondering when the next Dylan cover was coming along, or for a song that lasts under three minutes, wait no longer. Brought to their notice by Tom McGuinness and one of the songs that had appeared on *Lo and Behold* the previous year, 'Get Your Rocks Off' is another song from the basement tapes collection, part-grunge, partly blues-stomper. Not one of Dylan's best by any means, it's a repetitive stomper that yearns to follow in the footsteps of someone like Bad Company without quite succeeding, and lacks any obvious hook or tune.

The second instrumental, 'Sadjoy', follows along similar lines to 'Cloudy Eyes'. A slow, dignified theme that sounds rather like a funeral march, it has quite an appealing hook in the melody. Manfred originally wrote it, he said, for brass and strings, as a kind of exercise in 'playing a theme and having as much musical freedom as possible'. Mick's guitar leads are supported well by keyboards and a wordless vocal from Liza Strike, Ruby James and the band themselves that follows the tune, and the whole anticipates some of the slower theme-like numbers that Mike Oldfield would shortly make his own.

The blues song 'Black and Blue', which had been in their live set for some time, was written by two members of the Australian band Chain, about the deprivations and ill-treatment suffered by English convicts deported there and held in captivity in the subcontinent at the turn of the 20th century, breaking rocks in the chain gang. Being about injustice and an indictment of the system, it seems strange that it should have been not merely censored but actually excluded from the American release at the time for fear of giving offence. As a piece of blues it works well, Mick's guitar providing a powerful break after the first verse and chorus before Manfred takes centre stage with the Moog, at one point, the bass and drums being briefly faded out altogether before returning as part of a build-up towards the second verse. The whole track lasts close to seven minutes, with over half of it being taken up by the lengthy break at the centre and another after the second chorus to finish with.

For the final track, they return to the Dr John songbook. 'Mardi Gras Day' is a sunny, carnival-like calypso shuffle redolent of a celebration in the open air, with party noises adding to the atmosphere. It may be inconsequential, but makes for a light-hearted, optimistic way to close an album that has its fair share of weighty material. With its simple tune and the backing vocals, it sounds like everybody was having fun in the studio.

The bonus track, 'Pretty Good', was a song written by John Prine and recorded on his eponymous debut album, released in 1971. A cheerful country-folk tune in which the tune sits on three chords, the group transform it into an irresistibly commercial rocker that conjures up instant mental pictures of ZZ Top crossed with Status Quo. Only four minutes long, it sounds nothing like the rest of the album and would probably have cried out for single release, had it not been for one verse in dubious taste about a woman being raped by a dog. Several years previously,

Manfred had been careful enough to rearrange 'Just Like a Woman' and omit the second verse, which referred to amphetamines. It had admittedly been part of a song recorded for release as a 45, which they wanted to ensure did not risk being banned. Even so, it is remarkable that he should have allowed another contentious lyric to slip through a few years later. No less odd is the fact that it was accepted for the album in America by Polydor as a substitute for a song deliberately rejected as it dealt with the issue of slavery – albeit from a critical point of view.

Among the front rank of British music journalists, Chris Welch had become an eager champion of the group and was positive about their future direction. For him, the record showed that they now appeared 'to have shaken off all ties with the past and found a strong identity for themselves. The production is nicely adventurous, without over-indulging in too much gimmickry.'

As regards the original 1973 release, the fact that *Messin'* had seven tracks in all, three lasting between seven and ten minutes each, suggests that this was the start of Manfred Mann's Earth Band's prog era. At the time, it seemed almost obligatory for anyone who did not want to be pigeonholed as a hit singles band to ensure their albums either had only two or three lengthy cuts per side, or at least one marathon approaching the seven-minute mark, if not more. In this case, a frantic touring schedule with less time to spare in the studio and an inclination to make their material stretch out longer by including a lengthy jam or two – something they did regularly onstage – must have been an irresistible temptation.

'Get Your Rocks Off' was issued as a single on both sides of the Atlantic. Apart from its lack of any strong commercial hook, it fell foul of radio programmers everywhere. The title was basically slang for having an orgasm, and Manfred admitted the BBC were worried about it – 'it's a drag because it could easily have been a success.' In America, the Federal Community Bureau had recently been investigating drugs and payola in the music business, and decided the title must surely have drug connotations.

That summer, Manfred Mann's Earth Band played their first major British festival, at the London Music Festival at Alexandra Palace in London. It ran for ten days and they shared the bill on the final day, 5 August, with Uriah Heep, The Sensational Alex Harvey Band, The Gary Moore Band and The Heavy Metal Kids. The following week, they released the hit 45 that had so far eluded them. A place in the Top 10 was on its way, as was *Top of the Pops*. For their leader, it would seem like something of a throwback to the previous decade.

The Planets, an orchestral suite consisting of seven movements by Gustav Holst, was a particular favourite of Manfred, and he was keen to adapt part of the work for a future project. As it had been first performed in 1918, it was still in copyright, and permission had to be sought from the composer's daughter Imogen as executor of his estate. Manfred and Mick had already planned a song based on a movement from *Jupiter, the Bringer of Jollity*, part of the suite. Mick suggested they ought to record 'Make Your Stash', which he called 'a light-hearted Australian drug song', recorded two years previously by Australian group Spectrum.

The BBC would still think twice about broadcasting any song on radio or television that could be interpreted as encouraging or condoning drug use, and Manfred told him they ought to write their own version instead. They therefore based it on the original title, hence 'Joybringer', and the opening line, 'I bring joy.' Only when they had started recording it did they realise that it would be unwise to proceed any further until they had secured official approval. Fortunately for them, when Imogen Holst listened to a demo, she was favourably impressed and gave them her go-ahead. Spectrum had also given Gustav Holst a joint writing credit on their version, which suggested that they had also received official authorisation – unless they were prepared to go ahead without it and risk legal action. The song was completed and recorded that summer, credited jointly to Holst, Mann, Rogers and Slade. Colin loved the song and the arrangement so much that he named his boat after it.

By 1973, other groups who appealed to a similar audience, such as Focus, Roxy Music and The Strawbs, realised that releasing singles and promoting them on television (and not just on *The Old Grey Whistle Test*, then regarded as the more adult counterpart to *Top of the Pops*) did not necessarily mean that they were consigning artistic integrity to the four winds by selling out to a teen audience. More importantly, it could help them to tap into the more respectable, lucrative albums market. 'Joybringer' was released as a stand-alone single in August, playlisted by Radio 1, featured twice on *TOTP*, and peaked at No. 9 in September.

Manfred stressed that it was not really representative of their music, but it had at least brought them wider recognition with the public: 'It's just that the only way people become aware of your existence is by having a hit record. And that's our aim with this one.' They had been gigging regularly as the Earth Band for over two years and although they had always gone down well in Britain, they still felt like virtual unknowns: 'Nobody has taken any real notice of us.'

Lack of success and attention in their home country had rankled with them, and at one point, Manfred said that they thought very seriously about making their home in the United States, as that was increasingly the focus of their plans. As for singles, he acknowledged that making them was hard work, and he did not see them as continuing to put them out any more, as they would rather achieve respect as an album and concert band. Yet they would not be the only British band who would soon change their policy and find the strategy paid off in a musical climate where the division between singles and album-oriented acts was becoming far less marked. He admitted to being very pleased, 'but it won't alter anything within the band'. They regarded themselves as primarily a live rather than a recording unit, and yet in Britain, they were forced to play small gigs at the regular town, city, college and university venues. In Germany and other European countries, they had acquired much greater prestige as they were constantly in demand for the larger festivals. 'The whole thing is building,' he said, 'but in this country, nothing is really built.'

Part of the problem with Britain was that Manfred still felt he had not shaken off completely the pop image associated with his name. Playing in Europe was often more enjoyable as audiences weren't 'going back to the 1960s' and only knew them as the Earth Band. Nobody was expecting or shouting out for the old hits, 'they just listen to what we're playing'. Status Quo had buried their early psychedelic pop image, but only after exceptionally hard work on the live circuit as they gradually transformed themselves into a full-on rock 'n' roll, blues and boogie attraction with a few carefully spaced out hit singles that helped to launch their albums into major sellers. Manfred Mann's Earth Band were travelling the same path, but for them, it was taking a little longer.

'Joybringer' was the final track they recorded as part of their contract with Phonogram and the Vertigo label that summer. It left them free to join Gerry Bron's Bronze, for all territories worldwide except the United States and Canada. By this time, the next album was close to completion and would be available before the end of the year.

Solar Fire (1973)

Personnel:
Manfred Mann: organ, Mellotron, Minimoog synthesiser, vocals, lead vocals
(Earth, The Circle, Part 1)
Mick Rogers: guitar, vocals
Colin Pattenden: bass guitar

Chris Slade: drums
Additional musicians:
Irene Chanter, Doreen Chanter, Grove Singers: backing vocals
Paul Rutherford: trombone
Peter Miles: percussion
Producer: Manfred Mann
Studio: The Workhouse, Old Kent Road, London, 1973
Release date: November 1973
Chart placings: UK: – , US: 96
Running time: 37:10
Label: Bronze (UK), Polydor (US)
Side One: 1. Father of Day, Father of Night (Bob Dylan) 2. In the Beginning,
Darkness (Manfred Mann, Mick Rogers, Chris Slade) 3. Pluto the Dog
(Manfred Mann, Mick Rogers, Chris Slade, Colin Pattenden)
Side Two: 4. Solar Fire (Manfred Mann, Mick Rogers, Chris Slade, Colin
Pattenden) 5. Saturn, Lord of the Ring/Mercury, The Winged Messenger
(Manfred Mann, Mick Rogers) 6. Earth, The Circle Part 2 (Manfred Mann)
7. Earth, The Circle Part 1 (Claude Debussy, Manfred Mann)
Bonus tracks: Cohesion (1998)
8. Joybringer (Gustav Holst, Manfred Mann, Mick Rogers, Chris Slade) 9.
Father of Day, Father of Night (edited version) (Bob Dylan)

On what is often regarded by fans and critics as the group's most progressive album of all, *Solar Fire* continues the influence of Holst's *The Planets*. The estate prevented them from adapting any more of the original music. According to the notes that accompanied the 1998 CD reissue, about a double album's worth of material had been recorded in anticipation of permission being granted, and it was either scrapped or has long since disappeared. What emerged, as a result, was loosely identifiable as a single concept album, based on and inspired by the origins of the universe, the solar fire that set life into motion after the creation of the world, and the themes of Holst's work.

It was a pigeonhole that Manfred wasn't entirely comfortable with. 'I don't think in terms of theory and ideas,' he told Merrill Shindler of *Rolling Stone*. 'People say, "What do you do, conceptual albums?" and I answer, "No, just a bunch of songs." I'm kind of against ever explaining things that I do. My feeling is that everybody hears it how they hear it and I let them, without explaining why, what and where for. The answer is, really, "It sounds good."'

The first and longest track on the album has nothing to do with planetary inspirations. 'Father of Day, Father of Night' was the only track that none of them wrote, although they could certainly claim credit in rearranging it beyond all recognition to a mammoth work to around six times the length of the original. It began life in 1970 as a jaunty, apparently spontaneous song that appeared as the final track on Bob Dylan's *New Morning*. He had based it on his interpretation of a Jewish prayer, 'Amidah', and his version, which features only a single-take vocal and his piano as accompaniment, is just 90 seconds long. Three years later, Manfred transformed it into a majestic suite of massive proportions, with the phrase 'King Crimson meets Pink Floyd' or similar coming very much to mind. Other reviewers suggested the group were going into the realms of space rock alongside the likes of Hawkwind.

An ethereal intro is provided by the Grove Singers, a long-established chamber choir based in central London. Although they never appeared live with the group, tapes featuring their contribution were sometimes used onstage as necessary. This gives way to a bombastic burst on keyboards before a more soothing mini-symphony from church organ, Mellotron and guitar usher in the vocal section. As the lyric is very short, basically amounting to three verses repeated at intervals, much of the number is taken up with instrumental passages, inspired by sections from Holst's adagio movement from *Saturn, the Bringer of Old Age*. A very restrained, almost ambient section led by guitar is led into a more vigorous time signature by drums, while the keyboard work and choir return at intervals to herald another vocal section around seven minutes in. It eventually explodes into a powerful coda with all instruments up to the fade. For many years it remained an integral part of the group's live set, extended further by the interpolation with improvisation and sections from one or two other pieces. Some fans regard it as one of their masterpieces, an epic performance that they rarely surpassed on record during the rest of their career.

'By the time we finished with it, it was as much our song as Dylan's, I think,' Manfred told Jeff Ward in *Melody Maker*. 'I really don't mean that to sound arrogant, but there was so much concept put into the song, and yet we were basically using what I think is a lovely song.' His enthusiasm for the songwriter's work remained undiminished. He said that there were times when he would really like to stop doing Dylan numbers, but it was difficult for him as he kept hearing the songs and thought that nobody else had figured out how to arrange them differently from the originals. He thought that Dylan 'completely threw the song away' on *New Morning* by not having developed it to its full potential: 'You can't hear a song like that and let it go by.'

While 'Joybringer' was in the charts the previous year, Manfred said he had been thinking about another single that he had in mind, a number that he also planned to record as a ten-minute album track. A three-minute edit of 'Father of Day' was prepared, with the extended instrumental passage removed and replaced with a short guitar solo from Mick. It was issued as a 45 in Britain, America and most European countries, but without success.

On the recording, Manfred used a Mellotron, but it wasn't an instrument he favoured. Any band he heard using one, he insisted, sounded very muddy unless the Mellotron was playing on its own. 'When everyone's playing together, you've got this big orchestra going "Mmmmmmm".' As they had used it on the record, he decided to try it on one gig – for 15 seconds. It did not really work, and he never repeated the experiment.

After the majesty of the opening track, 'In the Beginning, Darkness' reverts to hard rock of Black Sabbath and Deep Purple proportions, and the closest the album gets to such territory. A vigorous drum pattern (including a brief solo) gives the pulsating guitar riffs a run for their money, while Mick comes close to Ian Gillan or Ozzy Osbourne territory on the vocals. After a couple of minutes, the backing vocals, drums and spacey synths take over, with some more funky guitar soloing before a repeat of the vocal section. A little over five minutes long, with minor editing, it might have been a better choice for a single.

Following two somewhat portentous works, as if to remind us that it can't be unmitigated deadly earnestness, they insert a short instrumental. Not quite three minutes long, 'Pluto the Dog' is a theme built over a pulsating bass and drums riff with Moog bending notes one moment and sounding like electronic pan pipes the next. In keeping with the title, a careful listen will reveal canine guest vocals at intervals.

Side two begins with the title track. An intro with organ, spacey synths and powerful guitar work lead into a song with impassioned vocals on a cosmic theme from Mick, supplemented by a call-and-respond routine from the Chanter Sisters.

The instrumental segue of 'Saturn, Lord of the Ring' and 'Mercury, The Winged Messenger', goes through several shifts of time signature. A slow, dignified early section drifts in and out of a relaxed pace that can best be described as a gentle blues shuffle, with the guitar alternately vigorous and laid-back. Such contrasts were designed to portray in musical terms the feeling of old age in the first part and the energy of youth in the second. More spacey synths come, go and return. In the final 90 seconds, all musicians go furiously into overdrive, reminiscent of the interplay by Ritchie Blackmore and Jon Lord on Deep Purple epics like 'Highway Star' and 'Fireball', for example. 'Saturn' had been conceived during the Chapter Three era and played at the Woods of Dartmouth Festival, Massachusetts, during their American tour in May 1970, but then mothballed and not fully developed until now.

The album concludes with two instrumentals (or should one say almost-instrumentals), 'Earth, The Circle Part 2, credited to Manfred, and 'Earth, The Circle Part 1', on which he shares the composing credit with Claude Debussy, whose *Jimbo's Lullaby* provided the main inspiration for the music. Both are a little over three minutes long. (Should those track titles not come in reverse order?)

'Part 2', which had started life as 'Bubblegum and Kipling' as a work-in-progress first recorded for a BBC Radio 1 session earlier that year, sounds to some extent like a continuation of the previous number. It opens with some synth doodling that sounds as if it has its roots in Celtic folk dance music, followed by a brief vocal section (two lines) and then a return to the heavy rock style with guitar and keyboards alternating. Finally, Part 1 is itself a work of two parts, the first a slow section featuring Manfred singing over a slow and stately backdrop of tinkling keyboards. After two minutes, it crossfades with a snappy jazz shuffle playing the same motif over and over again, like an old-fashioned music box or a piano that has been speeded up. It gradually crossfades with a return to obscured vocals that sound as if coming from some distance away.

There were minor differences between the British and American releases. The former included both parts of 'Earth, The Circle', while the stateside version only had the first part (and dropped 'Part 1' from the track listing), as well as the inclusion of 'Joybringer', despite failure to repeat its British chart success over there.

The album was released midway during an extensive tour of England that lasted from late October until the week before Christmas, the highlight of their schedule being a gig at the Golders Green Hippodrome, recorded by the BBC for a Radio 1 In Concert broadcast.

Interestingly, they didn't take the opportunity to showcase more than a fraction of the album. Their set list for the show comprised 'Mercury, The Winged Messenger', 'Buddah', 'Messin'', (both from the previous album), 'Father of Day, Father of Night', and 'Mighty Quinn'. 'Father', a performance that ran to over 16 minutes, interpolated parts of 'Captain Bobby Stout' and 'Glorified Magnified', with a heavier version of 'Mighty Quinn' from the chart-topper that had long since become a staple oldie on British pop radio. It had long been in the group's live repertoire as an encore, sometimes as part of a medley with 'Pretty Flamingo', and would remain so for many years yet. Manfred would introduce it with gentle irony onstage: 'For our last number, here's something I recorded back in 1967 – when I used to be a pop star.'

With its complex, lengthy tracks, *Solar Fire* dispelled any doubts about the group being anything other than a prog rock band, and reviews in the British music press at least were overwhelmingly positive. Some listeners hailed it as a masterpiece alongside contemporary releases by Yes, Emerson, Lake & Palmer and King Crimson, with *Melody Maker* hailing it as 'probably the most vital, integrated album they've produced to date'. 'Definitely an album for the more progressive music fan,' was *Record Mirror*'s verdict. 'In that particular sphere, it compares well with anything released over the last year.' A small minority dismissed it as pretentious, overblown nonsense that would age rapidly before the 1970s were out. Yet for a more open-minded audience, it demonstrated a remarkable fusion of hard rock, classically inspired fare, occasional touches of jazz, Manfred and Mick's flair for improvisation and little hints of quirky humour. More significantly, despite the Holst and Debussy inspiration and another Dylan song, albeit turned completely inside out, it was the record in which they had the greatest creative input with regard to composing credits.

In Britain, it sold steadily over a long period, ultimately reaching gold status although never appearing in the album chart. In America, it made the Top 100 briefly in May 1974, despite the lack of a hit single. Its best sales were throughout mainland Europe and Manfred believed that its release had taken them a step forward. Yet, in their home country, it was still hard for them to make that breakthrough. 'England seemed to find it harder to accept us, perhaps because there was a greater heritage from the past.'

Left: Tom McGuinness, Manfred's bandmate from the 1960s and occasional co-producer, onstage with McGuinness Flint at the Marquee, London, c.1973.

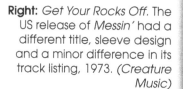

Right: *Get Your Rocks Off.* The US release of *Messin'* had a different title, sleeve design and a minor difference in its track listing, 1973. *(Creature Music)*

Left: The group, just as their British chart fortunes were about to improve, in 1973.

Right: *Solar Fire.* Sometimes seen as the group's most progressive album, partly inspired by the origins of the universe and the music of Gustav Holst from 1973. *(Creature Music)*

Left: 'Joybringer'. Sheet music for the Holst-inspired single that gave the group their long-awaited top ten debut, 1973.

Right: 'Father of Day, Father of Night'. French single picture sleeve, a three-minute edit of the Dylan-written album trackthat never charted but became a favourite in their live set, 1974.

1974

For much of the year, Manfred Mann's Earth Band were on the road, initially playing America throughout January and February, with Uriah Heep on some dates. March and the first week of April were taken up with a tour of Britain, after which they returned across the Atlantic for shows with Kiss and Savoy Brown, interspersed with a couple of gigs in Germany on a bill with Camel and Steeleye Span. The American jaunt between May and August found them playing alongside Blue Öyster Cult and Aerosmith. September was taken up with playing in Sweden, while in October and November, they were back in Britain. They returned to America for more gigs in December, sharing the bill on different nights with Brian Auger and the Oblivion Express, Rush, The J. Geils Band and The Sensational Alex Harvey Band.

During the American dates early in the year, they were convinced that things were really starting to happen for them, and in a way that had a considerable impact on the presentation of their music. In March, shortly after returning to England, Manfred told Jeff Ward of *Melody Maker*:

America has made a difference in our playing, now our playing will slowly settle back a little because we're recording, we're only playing weekends, we're not consistently on the road. But one of the main things about America is the realisation of how important it is as a market. We feel there's a chance they'll really turn on to us there in a big way, whereas I don't get that feeling here. A lot of bands go to America and it destroys them. They find the pressures very difficult. In some ways, obviously, the pressures are very high and things become more intense. But in our case, certainly, over the last years, it's been a big factor in our survival, this absolute confidence that things were going to go right in the States.

The Canadian gigs were also successful, although one problem later arose from their performances in the Ottawa-Hull area during the summer. Pre-recorded tapes were an essential part of the show and the promoter wrote to them afterwards, accusing them of using orchestral backing tracks. They responded that everything they played onstage was live, apart from taped effects they had created in the studio themselves, and it was entirely their own work. They weren't trying to 'fake their way', or trying to be an orchestra; they weren't doing any other musicians out of a job; and unlike several other bands, they never used orchestral walk-on tapes. To ensure that they were fully complying with regulations, they had since cleared matters with the American Federation of Musicians and received permission to carry on using them.

Their fifth album, *The Good Earth*, was released in October to coincide with the British tour. Whereas other contemporary acts were content to package their long players in lavishly designed gatefold sleeves with elegantly decorated booklets featuring the song lyrics, or give away free posters, they went one better. Every purchaser had the option to purchase a piece of land, one square foot of 'good earth' situated at Llanerchyrfa in the Abergwesyn Valley, Brecon, in South Wales. It was so difficult to locate that at the time it was said that only Chris Slade, a sub-postmaster, and the Forestry Commission knew exactly where it was. Many years later, the advent of the internet and Google Earth supplied the answer, with a map reference of 52 degrees 11' 06.39" N; 3 degrees 41' 54.59" W. The inner sleeve included a coupon printed on one corner that had to be sent in the post for registration, and several thousand fans did so by the closing date of 31 December 1975. Everyone who returned it received a documented freehold deed to the land. The offer was so popular that the Bronze Records office was overwhelmed with applications, and it was impossible to reply individually to all requests to advise of the plot number allocated. To satisfy public demand, an exhibition was set up in London where the information could be made readily available.

Manfred had bought the land through the Economic Forestry Unit earlier that year, apparently for about £1,000, and formed a company, Petbrook, to look after and administer it. He dismissed the theory that it was merely a gimmick to sell albums, 'as if anybody would buy a record they don't like just to get a free plot of land', and was quite annoyed by the negative reaction. His idea was to protect the land, and as so many people owned a part of it, it could not be sold. In spite of this, *The Good Earth* still did not sell enough to make the album chart.

Yet the idea was well ahead of its time in helping to bring general awareness of environmental issues to people's notice. In November 1995, the BBC marked the 21st anniversary of the scheme in a special edition of its weekly TV rural affairs programme *Countryfile*. As well as featuring interviews with Manfred and Mick, there was footage of a pilgrimage to the site in Wales made by long-standing fans from throughout Britain and Europe, as they took their original copies of the album to be autographed by the guitarist and vocalist who had been part of the project. Mick, complete with his electric guitar (strictly for the cameras, with no amp in sight), was also there to talk about the venture and meet the faithful. He said that even though the band knew that what they had done 'was a bit special', the response at the time caught them all by surprise. Fans pointed out that as they visited and walked around the area, they were struck by the fact that all the hillsides nearby had been taken over and planted out, mostly with conifers, by the Forestry Commission. They looked pretty, one of them said, but no longer natural. The original site had remained as nature intended it. 'You've got to keep places like this,' said another, 'otherwise they will just be covered over in concrete.'

Manfred had a less positive view of the experience and admitted that it scarred him. The journalistic profession had been utterly cynical in accusing them of trying to sell albums by giving away land, and he swore he would never do anything like that again. It was a response that might have been foreseen, but he was plainly disappointed that his motives had been interpreted in such a negative light.

The Good Earth (1974)

Personnel:

Manfred Mann: Hammond organ, piano, Hohner Clavinet, Minimoog synthesiser, keyboards

Mick Rogers: guitar, vocals

Colin Pattenden: bass guitar

Chris Slade: drums

Producer: Manfred Mann and Earth Band

Studio: The Workhouse, Old Kent Road, London, 1974

Release date: October 1974

Chart placings: UK: – , US: 157

Running time: 38:09

Label: Bronze (UK), Warner Bros (US)

Side One: 1. Give Me the Good Earth (Gary Wright) 2. Launching Place (Mike Rudd) 3. I'll Be Gone (Mike Rudd)

Side Two: 4. Earth Hymn (Manfred Mann, Chris Slade) 5. Sky High (Manfred Mann, Mick Rogers) 6. Be Not Too Hard (Mick Rogers, Christopher Logue) 7. Earth Hymn Part 2 (Manfred Mann, Chris Slade)

Bonus tracks: Cohesion (1998)

8. Be Not Too Hard (single version) (Mick Rogers, Christopher Logue) 9. I'll Be Gone (single version) (Mike Rudd) 10. Earth Hymn Part 2a (single version) (Manfred Mann, Chris Slade)

As the title and square foot of land offer both suggest, an ecological theme runs through part of this album, picking up to an extent where 'Messin'' on the third album left off. Elsewhere, there is a nod to all things celestial and universal, as if to pursue further the concept that inspired much of *Solar Fire*.

'Give Me the Good Earth' was a rearrangement of a song that had appeared as the opening track of *Footprint*, the solo album released in 1971 by Spooky Tooth keyboard player and vocalist Gary Wright. While the original was a straightforward three-minute number, the Earth Band rearranged it as an epic piece stretching out over eight minutes, the longest number on the album. Opening with the sound of a cockerel crowing, the song part is heralded by Mick's heavy bluesy guitar and impassioned vocal, while Manfred adds some off-the-wall synths. After about four minutes, most of the instruments fade out to leave some delicate drumming work as a soundtrack to the aural tapestry of countryside church bells, cattle, sheep and bird song. When the vocal returns, it sounds as if it is being phoned into the soundtrack. The pattern of light and shade continues with a reprise of the heavy guitar riffing and powerful rhythm section to match, until shortly before the fade-out that ends on a calm note with more countryside sounds.

It is followed by two songs by Mike Rudd of the Antipodean band Spectrum. 'Launching Place' starts with a bouncy synth, bringing to mind a piece of Celtic folk, as an intro to a mid-tempo song. This and the next one, 'I'll be Gone', verge on blue-eyed soul, with Mick sounding more like Steve Winwood.

Side two opens with the six-minute epic 'Earth Hymn'. From a tinkling xylophone at the start, it then becomes a colourful musical journey with seething guitar and a King Crimson-like Mellotron, with lyrics inviting the listener to a symphony of sound, 'drifting down through your dreams in an endless stream'. About halfway through, it speeds up to a frantic pace, culminating in reverse tape loops towards the fade.

The instrumental 'Sky High' sounds like a jam, with guitar and keyboards drawing from classical influences and a hint of jazz. The album's fastest tune, it barely eases up throughout a frantic five minutes. One might detect a hint of Santana in Mick's guitar work. One reviewer commented on the Zappa-like feel, suggesting that Manfred was not also influenced by him but also by the Mahavishnu Orchestra and Ornette Coleman, hence his attitudes towards the structural development and progression of some tracks. When this was suggested to him, he remarked on the fact that several of their tracks had sections in which they allowed themselves to improvise. 'There's a lot of freedom within very rigid arrangements. We try and get a kind of compromise between heavily arranged things and sections which are fairly loose, and all we know is how we're gonna get out of these things.'

'Be Not Too Hard' is a poem that had been written a few years earlier by poet, playwright and activist Christopher Logue. It had previously been set to music by Donovan Leitch and recorded as a single by Joan Baez in 1967. Mick regularly used to go to Manfred's house so they could informally practise songs that were under consideration for forthcoming albums. On one such occasion, he noticed a picture of a poem hanging on the wall in Manfred's kitchen, and liked it so much that he immediately jotted it down. When he got back to his apartment, he set the lines to music, and the next day he played it to Manfred, who was so impressed by what he had done that they started on an arrangement for it at once. It was the album's most commercial track and appropriately released as a single, although without any success. With its soothing lyric and powerful guitar and synth interplay, it sounds almost like a country number at one stage and a Christmas carol later on, with its pattern of chiming bells.

To conclude comes a reprise of the fourth track, 'Earth Hymn (Part 2)'. Mostly instrumental, it adds some deep Moog notes and tape effects this time around.

With its heavy reliance on the songs of others, interspersed with the eco-theme, at first, the album sounds like a rather uneven collection. Yet Manfred Mann's Earth Band were always ready to take chances, and, as ever, what may initially appear a rather scattershot helping of music coming from different directions proves an interesting listen, with several surprises on the journey to sustain interest throughout. In *Rolling Stone*, reviewer Ken Barnes gave it a mixed reception. He praised its 'economical playing' and for Mick's excellent vocals that he said sounded like an odd cross between Peter Gabriel and Steve Winwood. Yet he found himself 'impatiently enduring the instrumental segments waiting for the vocals' on some numbers, and feared that the Earth Band had lost its balance; 'only extensive concentration on tight vocal numbers can redress it.'

The release was followed by generous exposure on the BBC. In October, they were featured on *The Old Grey Whistle Test* performing 'Give Me the Good Earth', and the following month Manfred was interviewed by Alan Freeman on Radio 1's *Sounds on Sunday*, previewing and discussing the album. Yet such publicity, welcome as it was, clearly did little to raise the profile of the group or album much higher. Even though they had enjoyed one solitary top 10 hit just a year earlier, there was still no real substitute for getting a new single on to the weekly daytime playlist or a new release slot on *Top of the Pops*.

Above: *The Good Earth.* Purchasers of the album were offered 'rights over one foot of the earth' in the historic county of Brecknockshire, now part of Powys, Wales. 1974. *(Creature Music)*

Right: *The Good Earth.* A press advertisement for the album, including UK tour dates, autumn 1974.

Right: A day out on the river, c.1974.

Left: Mick Rogers onstage in 1974.

Right: A Christmas show at Ludwigshafen, Germany, also including Colosseum II, Steve Marriott's All Stars and Osibisa in 1975.

1975

The first three months of the new year found Manfred Mann's Earth Band with a full date sheet playing around England and Wales. In January, they played Imperial College, London, with Sutherland Brothers and Quiver, while on a tour during March and early April, they were supported by Clancy. Between the rest of April and May, they played several gigs in Europe, the majority in Germany with Climax Blues Band, where they had recently become very popular. In June, they shared a bill with Uriah Heep at one show at the Palais des Sports, Paris. Much of their time off the road was spent completing a sixth album, which would be the last from the original line-up. Manfred was also invited to play on a new rock version of Sergei Prokofiev's *Peter and the Wolf*, advertised with the strapline 'a symphonic fairy tale for children'. Narrated by Viv Stanshall, it included various rock luminaries, including Gary Brooker, Chris Spedding, Eno, Gary Moore, Phil Collins, Alvin Lee, Bernie Frost and Cozy Powell, as well as contemporary jazz-rock players Stephane Grappelli, Jon Hiseman, Henry Lowther, and Keith and Julie Tippett. Manfred added a Moog solo to the track 'Peter's Theme'.

For Mick Rogers, it would be a parting of the ways for a while. He had reached the stage where he was beginning to feel trapped by their limitations, and in his own words, 'wanted to stretch out a bit'. Having been a long-time admirer of Frank Zappa's music, he was in seventh heaven when the group had last played America in July 1974 and Zappa invited him to come and play bass at one show with his band at the Municipal Auditorium in Mobile, Alabama, when his regular player was unable to make it. Borrowing Colin's bass, he made the six-hour drive to busk his way through the two-and-a-half-hour set. The experience had made him keen to explore different musical territory in the Zappa and John McLaughlin mode, a direction that Manfred was not prepared to accommodate.

Manfred liked and admired the American musician and he owned some albums by The Mothers of Invention, but despite his love of musical experimentation and lifelong unashamed jazz leanings, he stressed that 'this is not what the Earth Band is all about', and made it clear that they would 'never sound like Zappa'. Feeling that there was no real opportunity for him to follow any such inclinations where he was, Mick began to become frustrated. In his words, 'I was becoming such a pest that Manfred called a band meeting and said, "Well, I'm sorry, Mick, but you will have to go, because you obviously want to do something else."'

Chris and Mick had always been very much kindred souls, and the drummer acknowledged how much he particularly appreciated his spontaneity.

He'd go off on a musical tangent and we'd follow. It was more like Cream if you can imagine, than anything else, and we'd always end up back at the starting point. And the records were trying to be more like Manfred Mann I think, than the original Manfred Mann, which was very successful, hunting for that hit. And I've always been better live than I am in the studio. In those days, Mick wanted to be John McLaughlin. I wouldn't have minded being Billy Cobham, but I don't think I had the chops. But Mick wanted to be a jazzer. And it was very apparent, and he became very, very disillusioned with the band after about five years.

It was to be an amicable departure born purely of diverging musical interests. Mick was invited to join Uriah Heep and then Colosseum II, whose jazz-rock style would have presumably fitted his aspirations well, but he declined both. The Colosseum vacancy went to Gary Moore, while Mick returned to Australia for a while and formed the jazz-rock outfit Eclipse. He subsequently returned to Britain and put Aviator together with former Jethro Tull drummer Clive Bunker. Yet as time would show, Manfred's break with Mick was to be anything but a permanent one.

The final gig of the original Earth Band line-up took place at the Amphitheatre, Chicago, on 22 August, and their final TV appearance on the Dutch programme *TopPop*, playing 'Spirits in the Night', was shown a month later. It coincided with the release of the next album, *Nightingales and Bombers*. The title came about because of a recording they had come across, made in a wood in Surrey on the night of 19 May 1942 by a BBC sound engineer who had intended to capture the song of nightingales in the countryside. Nearly 200 RAF bombers, including Wellingtons, Hampdens, Lancasters and Halifaxes, were flying overhead on their way to launch a raid on Mannheim, Germany, at the time, and they were also picked up on the tape.

Manfred admitted afterwards that the album was a difficult one to make. One reason was that the recording process resulted in a large number of audible tape splices that had to be sorted, the other being Mick's feeling increasingly at odds with their musical approach and needing to compromise with the others on the jazz-rock content, which in spite of their leader's jazz background they were less keen to embrace. Manfred himself also foresaw that a change in personnel was on the horizon. 'We really were reaching the end of where we were going,' he said. 'Towards the end of the album, we were thrashing around in the dark.' Significantly, much of Mick's guitar style on the record reflected his recent listening to the likes of the Mahavishnu Orchestra and Weather Report, and the result turned out to be the bandleader's most jazz-influenced work since the last Manfred Mann Chapter Three album.

Despite these problems, it marked the beginning of a significant step forward towards acceptance on both sides of the Atlantic. During one of their American tours, Manfred had met Ed Sharkey, a radio disc jockey in Philadelphia. He handed him a copy of a debut album by a songwriter who looked like a name to watch in the future, and told him he simply had to listen. The record in question was *Greetings from Asbury Park, N.J.*, by Bruce Springsteen. Curiously, it was another British name from the 1960s who had also just discovered him and was keen to help popularise the work of the as-yet little-known performer who would become New Jersey's greatest musical export. Allan Clarke had introduced the rest of The Hollies to his music not long before, and they released their own version of 'Sandy (4th of July, Asbury Park)' as a single in the spring of 1975, to some British interest and airplay but poor sales, and he would do likewise with 'Born to Run' in October as a solo 45 that year. It was unfortunate timing, as the latter hit the shops on the same day as Bruce's own recording as a single. Such head-to-head competition doubtless contributed to neither becoming a hit in Britain, although radio stations gave generous airtime to the writer's own rendition and Allan Clarke's passed virtually unnoticed.

Manfred was especially taken with two of the songs on *Greetings*, both of which had been singles in America, although neither were successful. They were hurriedly written to order and recorded at the behest of Clive Davis, boss of Columbia Records, who was very impressed with the album when tapes were initially delivered but said he could hear no potential hits on it. Over the next few years, the Springsteen songbook would provide Manfred Mann's Earth Band with almost as many cover versions as Dylan had done in the past. Meanwhile, both of these songs would be hits in America and one in Britain – not for the writer, but for the band who had taken to his work in such a big way.

Nightingales and Bombers (1975)

Personnel:

Manfred Mann: Hammond organ, synthesisers

Mick Rogers: guitar, vocals

Colin Pattenden: bass guitar

Chris Slade: drums

Additional musicians:

Ruby James, Doreen Chanter, Martha Smith: backing vocals

David Millman: viola

Chris Warren-Green: violin

Nigel Warren-Green, Graham Elliott, David Boswell-Brown: cello

Producer: Manfred Mann's Earth Band

Studio: The Workhouse, Old Kent Road, London, 1975

Release date: August 1975

Chart placings: UK: – , US: 120

Running time: 38:09

Label: Bronze (UK), Warner Bros (US)

Side One: 1. Spirits in the Night (Bruce Springsteen) 2. Countdown (Manfred Mann) 3. Time is Right (Manfred Mann, Chris Slade, Mick Rogers) 4. Crossfade (Manfred Mann, Chris Slade, Mick Rogers, Colin Pattenden)

Side Two: 5. Visionary Mountains (Pam Nestor, Joan Armatrading) 6. Nightingales and Bombers (Mick Rogers) 7. Fat Nelly (Manfred Mann, Peter Thomas) 8. As Above, So Below (live) (Manfred Mann, Chris Slade, Mick Rogers, Colin Pattenden)

Bonus tracks: Cohesion (1999) 8. Quit Your Low Down Ways (Bob Dylan) 9. Spirits in the Night (single version) (Bruce Springsteen)

The American version of the album, on Warner Bros, includes 'Quit Your Low Down Ways' as track six, making it slightly better value than the British release on Bronze. It had been recorded at the request of Warners, who felt that four instrumentals out of eight tracks was too many and another song would redress the balance a little.

The group introduced their fans to Bruce Springsteen on the opening track with 'Spirits in the Night'. In an expansive six-minute arrangement, Mick sings the verses in a relatively laid-back style, while going into full dramatic mode for the choruses. The backing vocal trio add some call-and-respond routines about three minutes in, and a fairly restrained break takes over about three minutes in. All guns are blazing by the time of the next chorus, which leads to the last verse with synth taking over at the end, just before the unaccompanied vocal line that completes the whole track. The full six-and-a-half-minute work was edited for single release to about half the length (while Bruce's own single was five minutes long, identical to his album track). In association with commercial radio stations London Capital, Glasgow Clyde, Manchester Piccadilly and Sheffield Hallam, Bronze Records promoted the single release in several British cities with a balloon race theme, each (toy) balloon carrying a postcard that allowed the finder to claim a prize of a copy of the single or album. Similar activities focused on the record, linking up with radio stations and pop magazines, took place in Europe and America. Yet like the 'own a piece of Welsh land' scheme launched by the previous album, chart action bypassed the record once again. The single reached No. 97 in America but failed everywhere else.

Although record buyers presumably took little if any notice of the lyrics, the song undoubtedly had more resonance in America. It includes various place names, including Greasy Lake, said to be a fictitious location based on two areas of water that Bruce and the members of his band used to visit regularly, while Route 88 is a road that goes through Ocean County, New Jersey. The title refers to 'greasers', vernacular for the local homeless who were referred to more poetically as 'gypsy angels', or even 'spirits in the night'. On American but not British releases, the song retained Bruce's original title in the singular, being listed as 'Spirit in the Night'.

'Countdown', the first of the instrumentals, is a short, brisk tune, with jazzy synth work and a brief drum solo. It leads into 'Time is Right', basically a rewritten version of 'Driva Man', an early 1960s jazz number written by composer and drummer Max Roach and lyricist Oscar Brown Jr. The Paul Jones-fronted Manfred Mann had covered the song on their EP *As Was* in 1966 and it had been part of the Earth Band's repertoire during their 1974 tour. As the lyrics, like those of 'Black and Blue' on the third album, dealt explicitly with the themes of slavery and civil rights, in order to avoid courting controversy, they substituted their own lyrics. A new arrangement differed sufficiently from the original number for them to be able to credit it as a group original. As a song, the structure is close to that of a 12-bar blues, with the added twist of a difference in pitch for one verse prior to the instrumental break. An organ-led passage builds to a dramatic break with frenetic keyboards and guitar jamming together before an ambient, chilled-out section reminiscent of Pink Floyd that then launches into the final verse, concluding with a dramatic finish on the last unaccompanied vocal line with heavy echo.

A second instrumental, 'Crossfade', is dominated by stuttering guitar and keys, significantly sounding rather like a Frank Zappa studio jam. More than any other track on the album, this showcases Mick's jazz chops and demonstrates how keen he was to pull the group in such a direction.

On 'Visionary Mountains', as on 'Father of Night' two years previously, the group show how a very short song (in this case, a mere fragment of fewer than two minutes) can be developed and taken to near-epic proportions with a more ambitious arrangement. Co-written by Joan Armatrading and Pam Nestor, it initially appeared on the former's 1972 debut, *Whatever's For Us*. A number with the message of 'love and the longing to survive', the group pack plenty of drama into five and a half minutes with a heavy guitar solo, followed by softer organ work, and a call-and-respond vocal routine between Mick and the trio.

The title track, and the only number credited solely to Mick, gives him a chance to stretch out on an instrumental that fuses jazz and new age sounds, again with plenty of light and shade. A quiet, restrained opening with melodic guitar line laid over a complementary bass figure then takes flight as the synth and drums build up into an attacking jazzy rhythm and hits what sounds like a dramatic finish, then returns to the beginning for a reprise of the initial melody, for a graceful final 80 seconds or so.

'Fat Nelly' is a rather sinister lyric credited to Manfred and Peter Thomas. The two verses, both repeated, tell of a woman who was killed with a butcher's knife, while a rape takes place by a garden gate. Fortunately, the majority of the number is taken up not by this grim tale but with chopping organ style, sounding as if it is in direct descent from the intro to The Who's 'Won't Get Fooled Again' and a similar organ sound would resurface on their greatest hit around a year later. All the same, it remains one of their less interesting numbers.

Recorded live, although with no evidence of audience sounds to be heard, 'As Above So Below' completes the original release. Yet another instrumental, quite fast-paced, with heavy guitar and keyboards in the background, it fades to leave a final minute of the bomber command planes and bird song from which the album took its title. Why they were not used on the title track instead remains unexplained.

Initially available only on the vinyl release, on 'Quit Your Low Down Ways', they invest the Dylan song with some distinctive bluesy guitar licks, similar to Manny Charlton's work with Nazareth at the time.

Although it would not have been hit single material any more than their version of 'Please Mrs Henry' ever was, it is still a spirited performance.

As far as some of the media were concerned, the record was a noticeable advance on its predecessors. *Sounds* remarked in its review that after what it called 'a trio of somewhat unremarkable albums for Phonogram, the Earth Band seemed to draw strength from a new contract with Bronze and have set about producing music of a considerably more substantial and interesting nature.'

To replace Mick Rogers, Manfred recruited not one new member, but two. Vocalist and rhythm guitarist Chris Thompson, who was born in England but brought up in New Zealand, had worked with groups in his adopted country, but none of them achieved lasting success. Initially, he was known as Chris Hamlet Thompson (hence a credit as such on the next two albums), as there was another well-known singer named Chris Thompson in New Zealand. By a remarkable coincidence, both performers with such similar names were neighbours for a while.

On returning to England, Chris auditioned unsuccessfully as vocalist for Argent, who were looking for someone to replace the recently departed Russ Ballard, then answered an advertisement in *Melody Maker*: 'Band with deal needs guitar player/singer, no time wasters.' It involved taking a cassette of his voice, knocking on a door, handing Manfred the tape and going home. A call followed, asking if he could come and do an audition. Out of all the eager hopefuls who had submitted tapes, his stood out head and shoulders as the best. 'I think I had about ten (auditions),' he recalled. 'Manfred finally begrudgingly told me that I had the job.' Any momentary coolness, it was suggested, might have been because by strange coincidence Chris was wearing, a Frank Zappa T-shirt. Naturally, he was not to know what an ironic choice that turned out to be. Fortunately for everyone involved, he did not have Mick Rogers' all-consuming devotion to the American icon, and was also a keen admirer of Springsteen.

Looking back some 40 years later, Chris talked in an online interview about his times with the group and their leader's remarkable work ethic. They played – or rather worked – five days a week from 11:00 in the morning till 7:00 at night, he said, with a break for lunch, rehearsing maybe four or five songs a day for concerts and recording purposes. Manfred was a hard taskmaster and he drove himself hard as well. 'Going on the road was fantastic, but it was very gruelling. You never knew when you were going home!' Yet he had the utmost admiration for their workaholic of a leader, as later revealed in a YouTube interview.

A person who's had Manfred's amount of success, followed by success all over again, just has to be someone special. You may want to go down to the shops; he just wants to go over an arrangement again. He's always talking about the music. But working with him is always a laugh. He's not at all bossy. He analyses himself in the same way he analyses other people. He recognises his own mistakes. He's always willing to listen.

Chris was a vocalist and rhythm, not lead, guitarist, and Manfred found it necessary to expand the group to a quintet. The new lead guitarist Dave Flett, from Scotland, had played with various local groups in the Aberdeen area. He lived in London for a while and was working as a laundry van driver when told about the vacancy by a friend who worked at the Workhouse Studio and recommended he ought to apply.

Introducing two members into a group that had had the same line-up for four years was quite an upheaval, and Manfred admitted he was cautious about the change. He said he always needed to be absolutely sure before he got up to do something, that it really was the right solution. 'It's the same with an album. My belief is that the first ten gigs any band does will be duff, yet I believe now, listening to us at rehearsal, that my caution has been unnecessary. When you play onstage, you really put yourself on the line. Anyone has got the right to get up, turn his back on you and walk out – which is an insult, because you're playing and he's walked out on you. That's why I don't ever want to play in a band that's no good live.'

With the two new members, he foresaw a change in musical emphasis. While they had been around 80 per cent instrumental in Mick Rogers' day, with so much reliance on improvisation, now he expected they would be closer to 60 per cent instrumental work, with correspondingly more emphasis on vocals in future. When he spoke to others around him, they confirmed his feeling that they were now becoming melodic, with more songs and slightly less instrumental. A lot of people told him that it had finally come together after inconsistencies and schizophrenia. 'To some, the schizophrenia is still there, because there has always been a jazz-rock element, and the straight song element.'

When he had formed the Earth Band at the beginning of the decade, he suggested to Gordon Coxhill of *NME* that he appreciated the idea of having a stable personnel with which to work. Every time he embarked on something new, he said, he always thought of it as being permanent.

> I could never have subscribed to that idea about fluid groups moving around and all the time jamming here and there. To me, that would be totally depressing. I like to have something organised and I work with people I have got confidence in. Each change I have made has been a natural change.

The four-piece line-up had endured for five years and six albums, but they would never have the luxury of such stability again. Chris Slade also commented on the changes the new line-up made to the band on YouTube.

> The lead singer and guitarist at the same time gone, and we're down to a three-piece with Manfred, who can't sing or not very well, sings about as well as me, and the bass player and drummer. So that's when Chris Thompson and Dave Flett came in. And it became a different band, of course, but there were two guitarists now, which gave another dimension.

Saying goodbye to one member and integrating two replacements might have been a daunting one at first, but soon came to be seen as a natural enough change. The new five-piece line-up held several rehearsals before resuming dates in America from the end of September, with a few more appearances in England and Germany during the last few weeks of the year.

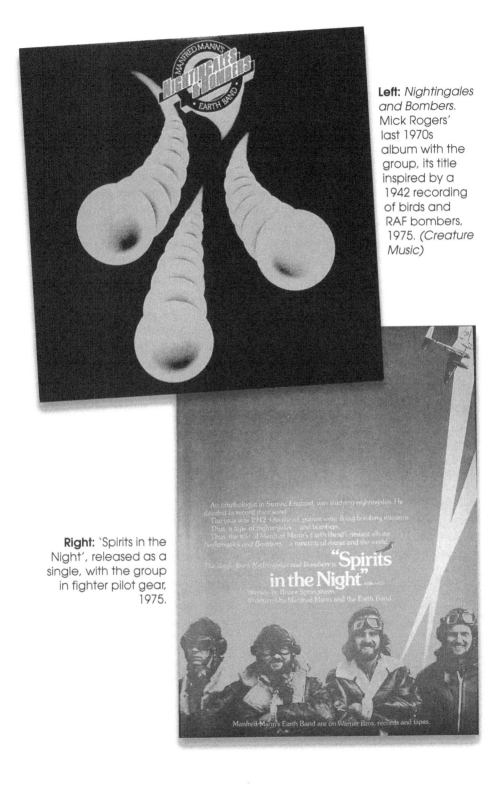

Left: *Nightingales and Bombers.* Mick Rogers' last 1970s album with the group, its title inspired by a 1942 recording of birds and RAF bombers, 1975. *(Creature Music)*

Right: 'Spirits in the Night', released as a single, with the group in fighter pilot gear, 1975.

1976

For Manfred Mann's Earth Band, 1976 would follow a similar pattern to that of the two previous years, with a new album to be completed and released, plus several dates in Britain, America and Europe. It would also be the year that a new single would not only set the charts alight, but also bring them the major album success they had long sought.

From February until the beginning of May, they played several gigs in England, mostly at colleges, universities and polytechnics, with one in Germany and also what would turn out to be Manfred's final show at the Marquee Club in London. When asked by Chris Welch whether he still enjoyed being on the road after all these years, he admitted that despite the drawbacks of arriving home at 5 a.m. afterwards, after having been existing on greasy motorway food eaten in a hurry, he preferred it to being in a studio all the time. 'The good thing about being on stage is that you are taking a chance every time you get on. You have immediacy, and that's what music is. If you're making records, you're using technology. Now we spend more and more time making the records than we used to. You have to get that right because it's what people take home with them.'

Playing live, he told Graham Neale of *Way Ahead* magazine, was the only thing he relished, or at any rate, found preferable to slaving over their next offering on vinyl.

I don't like recording, although I think we are getting the albums right now. This band has always been good live and it was the albums we needed to work on. We thought we could rely on the live gigs, but I realised a couple of years ago, that that wasn't true, but I still don't like recording. I don't like being locked in a studio with its technological atmosphere around me. The studio is a place that is almost designed to prevent you from playing music with feeling and you always have to search for the inspirational moment, so I really enjoy playing live gigs, it's very important to me personally.

At the end of August, they were at last added to the bill at the three-day Reading Festival over the Bank Holiday weekend, playing on Saturday as part of a line-up with Eddie & The Hot Rods, The Pat Travers Band, Camel, Van Der Graaf Generator, Jon Hiseman's Colosseum and Rory Gallagher. Manfred regarded it as 'a milestone to them' as it was their first such event in England during their five-year history, and it confirmed his belief that they really did have an audience in Britain. The albums were selling well, 'not superstar status', but there was at least a groundswell of enthusiasm for them, proved by attendance at gigs and subsequent positive audience reaction.

Until then, he admitted, his attitude had been one of 'forget England, I'm not bothered, as the press and publicity here have virtually ignored us for a few years and everywhere else we were doing well'. Since then, everything had gradually 'come right here', and he didn't feel resentful. But it struck him as strange that they were playing well, going down a storm everywhere else they appeared, and yet they weren't offered one festival in their own country, anywhere on the bill. Because of that, his vote was against playing the Reading Festival unless they could do so at a better time. 'As it turned out, it was good, so I was proved wrong.'

That Saturday at Reading would be remembered by others for a different reason, and not necessarily the right one. During torrential rain, while they were onstage, the sound cut out for a while. John Peel, who was compering the weekend's proceedings, racked his brains to think of some way to keep the crowd entertained until normal service was resumed. He, therefore, suggested that the crowds should let off steam by shouting, 'John Peel is a cunt!' They responded, he later noted in his autobiography, 'with considerable verve at once and several more times during the evening.' It later resulted in complaints from residents over four miles away.

The new five-piece line-up had helped them by heralding a positive change. Manfred was sure that members' attitudes within the band had become more open, less self-conscious, as he told Richard Green in *NME*. 'There was a schizophrenic element before, half jazz and half rock. Now I think we can combine the two. Chris is not, as Mick Rogers was, primarily a guitarist, but a vocalist. The way we perform alters the character of the band.'

It had made no difference to Manfred's constant quest for suitable material by other writers. While at home, he never ceased to listen to album after album by other artists, not for personal pleasure but for professional reasons. It was by no means a source of unbounded joy and he admitted it could be responsible for 'an immense degree of boredom', but despite that, he found it a good way of looking for and discovering new material by chance that was worth arranging for the group to record on a future album. He listened to obscure stuff, as he could often hear a song, or rather things in a song, that nobody else could. His brain, he admitted to Hugh Fielder in *Sounds*, never stopped working on material, and not just his own.

> If I'm driving through the country to go for a walk with my kids, I'm listening to Radio Caroline and if there's a track that sounds good, I'll sit until the end and find out who it is. If I'm in a fish and chip shop and something good comes on and I don't know who it is, I'll ask. If I go to South Africa to see my parents, I'll go into a record shop and see what's there because there might be a good writer. I never stop looking. I listen to so much and do so little. Rearranging is what I do best; seeing something from a different angle. I don't think any of us in the band writes stuff as good as the material I rearrange.

As for the matter of accumulating a huge, unwieldy record collection at home – he didn't care for the idea. Not being methodical about putting them in any kind of order, and hating the idea of living somewhere with walls full of albums that he never played, he readily gave them away to friends once they had served their purpose.

He now sensed that they were about to reach a new level of acceptance, and it would only take one track. The song that was about to unlock so many doors for them was a second Bruce Springsteen number taken from the *Greetings from Asbury Park* album. Chris Thompson also owned a copy and had been similarly bowled over by the music of the figure everyone would soon call 'The Boss'; 'I absolutely thought it was amazing. I thought this guy was fantastic and, obviously, Manfred saw a lot of worth in him too.' Even so, recording the number would prove a difficult task for them all.

Manfred spent a long time 'fiddling' with the arrangement of the song he had worked out. The original version he devised 'was very long and elaborate', quite different from the one that would eventually appear on record. When he had completed his first attempt, he played it on piano to the group as he hummed the melody. As one, they told him, 'I don't think it's us.' He put it aside, and it occurred to him 'that if we cut out the stopping and starting at the end of every verse then we could get somewhere. I knew there was some magic in it, particularly at the end with the two voices singing the verse and chorus together.' When they heard his new idea for the song, they were much more enthusiastic and agreed that was the solution.

'When we finally finished the album track,' Manfred said, 'I thought it had a great vibe, but the next question was how to get that into a single. The real problem was how to get from the chorus to the verse smoothly.' For a long time, he tried and failed to find the right way. 'And then – and this is why you need to be in a band,' Manfred said, 'Chris Slade suggested he ought to play "Chopsticks" over it.' They had already done that in the song, and Manfred was adamant that it could not work, but Chris's insistence persuaded him otherwise. He realised that Chris wasn't hearing 'Chopsticks' itself, just the chords, which fitted perfectly. So they recorded them as backing vocals and added that to the original. This was in the days when producers needed to try and lock two tape machines in tandem, a time-consuming process, but their efforts paid off.

Manfred omitted a couple of verses from the original, preferring to repeat two of the earlier ones instead, and thus omitted part of what he thought was the more surreal wordplay. Bruce had initially written the lyrics with a rhyming dictionary beside him, resulting in a cascade of words that called some of Bob Dylan's earlier songs to mind, notably 'Subterranean Homesick Blues'. Some years later, when he was talking about 'Blinded by the Light' to a television audience, Bruce advised viewers with a smile, 'Don't overthink the whole thing.' It was only a song, after all.

Once the musical arrangement had come together, one line in the lyrics proved more troublesome than the rest. Manfred had learned the song up to a point, but overlooked a certain detail. 'I find that if you keep referring back you can get over-familiar with it and start to think it's better than your lousy version,' he said. His copy of *Greetings From Asbury Park* did not have any lyrics on the sleeve, and with no internet or any other easy way to verify the words to a song, apart from spending ages trying to decipher them by listening repeatedly to the vinyl. If they misheard anything due to faulty diction, too bad.

The whole band sat around for several hours doing their best and eventually, they worked out that one line sounded like 'revved up like a deuce' (a deuce coupe, or car). Because of a minor technical glitch involving the angle of the tape head on the tape machine when they recorded their version, it had become very sibilant and sounded as if Chris Thompson was singing 'wrapped up like a douche'. They did not realise the extent or consequences of the problem until Warner Bros in America contacted Manfred to say they couldn't persuade radio stations in the southern Bible Belt to play the record 'because everyone thinks you're singing about a vaginal douche'. Some tweaking was in order.

Nevertheless, it probably helped the record in a way. Manfred thought it was funny how people would come up to him later and say, 'You know why that record was such a hit, don't you? Because everyone was trying to figure out if it was "deuce" or "douche".' Bruce Springsteen was also hugely amused by the controversy. When interviewed about the song on a programme in the *VH1 Storytellers* series, he remarked, 'One version is about a car, the other is about a feminine hygiene product. Guess which the kids liked to shout more?' It was suggested by some that Bruce hadn't been impressed at first with Manfred's version of his song, but later warmed to it – perhaps after he had seen a corresponding improvement in his royalty statements. It was, however, beyond dispute that he had always had much respect for Manfred Mann and his music, and from time to time, he included 'Pretty Flamingo' (admittedly not a Mann original, although they had made it famous) in his live sets. Manfred was told by 'somebody who knows Springsteen, I gather he finds it quite interesting what we've done – I don't know whether he likes it.'

It may or may not have been fortuitous that Manfred never realised his official plan to get Bruce to sing one of the two lines at the end of the song, combining the verse and the chorus. Not wanting the time-consuming business of going through managers or publishers, he found the number of the hotel where Bruce was staying while on tour and simply called him. Although it was mid-morning in America, he had probably had a late night. A very sleepy voice answered, 'Uh huh?' Manfred asked, 'Oh, are you a bit tired?' and the only response was a grunt. Manfred said he would call back. 'But I lost my bottle and I couldn't phone again. It's a shame, he'd have been great for it.'

Notwithstanding his admission that he wasn't really a great vocalist, he did the end section himself instead. 'You needn't be a good singer to sing a little bit, but you need to be a good singer to sing all the while,' he told Bob Edmands in *NME*, adding teasingly with a sidelong glance at his vocalist sitting beside him, 'In this case, my voice was a good contrast to Chris Thompson's unpleasant, gruff, big hero voice.'

When it came to recording songs written by others, he confessed to feeling no qualms about modifying the lyrics as appropriate. 'I'm quite happy to do that,' he told Merrill Shindler of *Rolling Stone*. If you listen to "Blinded by the Light", I've taken out words, I haven't been very honest to the original at all. I think that's quite important.' When Greg Russo asked him if he had tried to improve on Bruce's own version, he answered categorically that the original record was irrelevant. He was just trying to make his own record, not improve on the original, as there was no way in which it could really be bettered. 'It was just good material to work with. It's like getting a piece of stone if you're a sculptor.' He admitted that he had got some of the chords wrong, but in spite of that, he had reshaped it by adding some interesting touches, like a little jazzy run and a piano part that he confessed he had 'kind of stolen from Supertramp'.

Even so, the song proved exceptionally hard work to record. In a radio interview with Pete Feenstra, Manfred admitted that by the time he had completed it, he never wanted to hear it again. One day he decided to test the result by putting it on some speakers as background music while he was at home, at fairly quiet volume, and it sounded to him like an obvious failure, as it had 'no groove at all'. Then he had a phone call from Mike McGear, who had just heard a demo, and he said he was sure it would be a big hit in America. His instant reaction was that it was very polite of Mike to say so – but some people just had no ears. Nevertheless, others agreed that it had great potential, and second thoughts prevailed. The number that they had painstakingly recorded with the idea that it would be just another fairly lengthy album track would go on, once shortened a little, to provide them with their greatest hit ever.

In Britain, the edited version was released as a single at the beginning of August and received a positive review in *Melody Maker* from Caroline Coon, in the form of a letter to Bruce: 'Manfred doesn't stray too far from your original feel. The single rings out, gathering power and volume like an echo ricocheting around a vast Gothic tabernacle.' It went straight on to the Radio 1 playlist and was chosen as a record of the week by David Hamilton on his weekday afternoon show. Commercial radio stations and appearances on *Top of the Pops* followed suit, and it peaked at number six.

The Roaring Silence reached the shops at the end of the month. After six albums that sold moderately well over a period of time but never charted, the seventh took them into the Top 10 with what would be their highest position ever in Britain. As Manfred told Chris Welch in *Melody Maker*, it was nice to have a single in the charts, but the far more important thing was for it to generate interest in the album as well. Another tour had just been scheduled, and the timing was just right. 'Actually, it's a big stroke of luck because most people put out a single and album and do some gigs at the same time, and if the single doesn't happen, then it doesn't add up to much.'

The Roaring Silence (1976)

Personnel:

Manfred Mann: keyboards, backing vocals, lead vocals, last verse of 'Blinded by the Light'

Chris Hamlet Thompson: lead vocals, rhythm guitar

Dave Flett: lead guitar

Colin Pattenden: bass guitar

Chris Slade: drums, percussion, backing vocals

Additional musicians:

Doreen Chanter, Irene Chanter, Susanne Lynch, Mick Rogers: backing vocals

Choir: Gillian Ainscow, Stan Bailey, Marilyn Bennett, Janet Bunting, Peter Cudmore, Hilary Farnborough, Laurence Holden, Graham Jenkins, Philip Keywood, Jacqueline Nicholls, Jeremy Paynton-Jones, Chris Sennett

Barbara Thompson: saxophone

David Culpan, Margaret Wood, Tony Rowell: recorders

David Millman: string arrangements

Derek Wadsworth: horn arrangements

Producer: Manfred Mann and Earth Band

Studio: The Workhouse, Old Kent Road, London, 1976

Release date: August 1976

Chart placings: UK: 10; US: 10

Running time: 39:55

Label: Bronze (UK), Warner Bros (US)

Side One: 1. Blinded by the Light (Bruce Springsteen) 2. Singing the Dolphin Through (Mike Heron) 3. Waiter, There's a Yawn in my Ear (Manfred Mann)

Side Two: 4. The Road to Babylon (Manfred Mann, Peter Thomas, Colin Pattenden) 5. This Side of Paradise (Manfred Mann, Peter Thomas, Colin Pattenden) 6. Starbird (Manfred Mann, Chris Slade) 7. Questions (Manfred Mann, Chris Slade)

Bonus tracks: Cohesion (1998)

8. Spirits in the Night (1977 version) (Bruce Springsteen) 9. Blinded by the Light (single edit) (Bruce Springsteen)

The first American pressing of the album featured the same track listing as its British counterpart. A reissue the following year with a blue cover added the new version of 'Spirit In The Night', featuring Chris Thompson's vocal replacing that of Mick Rogers, as track five.

The full seven-minute version of the song that gave the group a belated breakthrough opens side one with a chopping intro on the organ. Almost three minutes in, a slower tempo brings the pace down for a break featuring lead guitar and organ, the guitar building up the pace a little after a minute or so. Next comes the famous 'Chopsticks' routine on piano, as suggested by Chris Slade, followed by the descending four-note sequence again and another verse. Towards the end comes a counterpoint passage where verse and chorus are being sung simultaneously on different stereo channels, interrupted after a while by a cataclysmic whoosh that brings everything to a halt. The final vocal line by Manfred himself, the one he had originally hoped he could persuade Bruce to sing, concludes a busy but varied song that takes the listener through several changes. The more familiar edited single version loses just over three minutes from the middle section.

Mike Heron's contemporary folk ballad 'Singing the Dolphin Through' started life as a song on *Mike Heron's Reputation*, the self-titled debut album of 1975 from the group he formed after The Incredible String Band had disbanded the previous year. Manfred had known Mike for several years, respected him as a writer and was keen to record one of his songs. At eight minutes plus, this is the album's longest track. There are suggestions of an anti-war theme, with references to searching for peace, comrades in arms telling each other, 'I know you can't stand the fighting for one more night', and 'we'll see no more hostile flag'. Musically it remains respectful to the mainly acoustic original, with the addition of six minutes in of a bridge where everything stops except the synthesiser, making way for a 90-minute saxophone solo from Barbara Thompson carrying on to the fade.

Following two cover versions, the rest of the album consists of originals. 'Waiter, There's a Yawn in my Ear' is a jam performed and recorded live, then subsequently overdubbed. It starts with some subtle work on the drums before the Moog enters with plenty of note-bending. Everyone holds back for the first two minutes or so, but by around halfway through, everyone is fired up, until the last two minutes which are close to an all-out attack from all four, with some very stately Keith Emersonesque flourishes to finish off. But was the title inspired by the cover design, or the other way round?

A semi-biblical epic appears in 'The Road to Babylon', which they had been performing live for some months as a work in progress under the title 'Well, Well, Well'. Like The Melodians' reggae song of 1970, 'Rivers of Babylon', which Boney M would soon turn into one of the best-selling British singles of all time, it is loosely adapted from Psalm

137, concerning the plight of the Jewish people after the conquest of Babylon, several centuries before the birth of Christ. A choral introduction based on the psalm, sounding like a Gregorian chant, leads the way to the rhythm section, guitar and Moog, and vocals. In the other verses, there are images of war, with references to a golden helmet, 10,000 swords and 10,000 voices marching on the road to Babylon – and a golden ocean turning to fire with 10,000 ships on fire. A heavy guitar solo is followed by a brief fade around five minutes in, and another interlude from the choir with ambient sounds paving the way for a reprise of a verse and chorus, ending with a sudden cut in mid-air. At times it evokes the style of Pink Floyd and King Crimson again, in one of the most ambitious tracks they ever recorded.

'This Side of Paradise' opens with some tinkling synth as the overture to lyrics that tell dreamily of eyes 'watching skies with salt water rain' and the moon passing by. A slow, reflective piece, overall, it conveys a dark mood, lightened by restrained guitar and Moog that goes through several different shades and patterns towards the fade-out.

At three minutes long, 'Starbird', the album's shortest cut, is largely instrumental. Based partly on Igor Stravinsky's *Firebird*, an a cappella intro of around 40 seconds takes it into a brief bass and drums passage before the guitar and Moog passage build up. A brief crossfade of instruments brings a return of vocals and synths for the final minute or so.

The album ends on the loveliest song of all. 'Questions' is a delicate ballad that avoids the intricacies and more sophisticated structure of most of the previous songs. It started as a poem that Chris Slade had written, and he was so pleased with it that he showed it to Manfred. After a while, he told Chris that he had found a good musical match for it, and with a few nips and tucks, the words and music fitted perfectly. A heartfelt lyric addresses the dilemma and sadness of someone seeking answers:

They answered my questions with questions,
And they pointed me into the night,
And the power that bore me had left me alone,
To figure out which way was right.

Musically it is structured around a piano piece based on Franz Schubert's *Impromptu in G flat major*. Dave, in particular, found playing the song a challenge at first. When Manfred first presented it to him, he felt completely out of his comfort zone and unsure of what he could contribute, but he knew that these flirtations with the classics were a speciality of their leader, and he would undoubtedly benefit from watching how he would blend a classical piece with a modern-day tune. Once they had worked out how to play it, he realised that it 'certainly provided a pleasant contrast to their other tracks on the album, which were very much in the standard rock format.' Chris was always proud of the song and once said that when he later joined AC/DC, he suggested they should consider playing it. Presumably, with tongue in cheek, he added that they rejected it without telling him why.

In sales terms, the album would prove to be by far the most successful in the group's catalogue. As much a perfectionist as ever, Manfred commented modestly afterwards to Graham Neale that he was satisfied with it, though they had recorded so much during the sessions that they had to reject at least 25 minutes of music. And at last, any qualms that a Top 10 single might attract the teenybop audience seemed to have been laid firmly to rest. After one show on the tour, he was relieved to observe that 'they weren't the wrong audience tonight, and it's been a hit single for five weeks now'. He was delighted to see that the audiences were evidently into the album 'and they're the type we want'.

'Questions' was released as a single in November and made no impression. It would be the only A-side they ever released during the decade written or co-written by Manfred. In spite of this, in *Sounds*, Hugh Fielder opined that 'after a series of interesting but often inconsistent albums', they had come up trumps this time. 'If the inconsistent element hasn't been completely buried, there's enough positive thinking and style in evidence to quell any latent discontent.' He singled out the recruitment of Chris and Dave as a major positive, saying that it was clear they had 'given the band a much sharper, more aggressive edge', especially on 'Blinded by the Light'.

Being back in the top 10 of the British singles chart had boosted the group's profile, but as Manfred was well aware, that could have its negative side. Hugh Fielder asked him how it would be if he found himself as leader of 'a top pop group again with singles in the charts and the image of the band becoming as important as the music [they] were playing.' Manfred dismissed the danger, saying, 'It could only happen if we made it happen.' They could start selling records, but it wouldn't place them under any obligation to keep putting out commercial, accessible singles. It went without saying that he wanted them to be very successful, as he told Chris Welch:

If you make music, then you want it to reach a great many people, but it really depends what the music is that's reaching all those people. That's the key. Hopefully, if it's an album, then there's no big problem, but if it simply revolves around the fact that all people remember you for is the single, then I wouldn't like that.

When it was put to him that they were about to go out on tour, and the fact that they had a single in the charts would surely draw more people to the gigs, he conceded that he was anxious that some of the audience wouldn't be into the band, so much as aware of one song than of them as a group. Chris Slade, who was also sitting in on the interview, added that 'Blinded by the Light' was 'not really that kind of single'. Manfred added that they had been in a similar situation not long before, when 'Joybringer' was doing so well, and they suddenly found kids in the audience screaming at them again. 'It only happened at a few gigs, but it was enough to make my blood run cold. It was like hearing a wolf cry in the middle of the night and not having a fire.' Probably because of this, not for many years did Manfred feel comfortable about playing the song live. Only after frequent requests did the group start doing so in 1991 during warm-up gigs, but Manfred and Mick were unhappy with the way it was presented live. They dropped it until 1993, when they reintroduced it as an instrumental bridge to the opening number, at that time their version of Bob Dylan's 'Shelter From the Storm'. But 'Blinded by the Light' remained a hardy perennial on the setlist.

As Hugh remarked, fans were unlikely to see Manfred guesting onstage with The Bay City Rollers, who had dominated the British singles and album charts for the best part of two years. However, he was a staunch defender of the group whom almost everybody over the age of 14 professed to hate at the time, telling Graham Neale that he felt 'almost aggressive' about the fact that the world was against them.

It's full of people who are resentful that these guys are being successful. Why the hell shouldn't they be, as this is what music is all about? I don't enjoy what they do, but that is no reason to knock them. I almost dressed up in a Rollers outfit for TOTP, but I thought that people might misunderstand.

For the rest of the year, the band were back on the road. After a gig at Cardiff Castle supporting Queen on 10 September, *The Roaring Silence* tour took to the road the next day, with Racing Cars as support, to do 17 dates until the beginning of October. A review of the final night at the Victoria Palace by Clive Bennett in *The Times* on 4 October provided a rather lukewarm appraisal of what he had seen and heard. He praised their 'considerable technical expertise', but noted that 'though there was plenty of variety in textures and rhythms, there was little sense of musical exploration'. As a result, 'the reprises of the strong melodies of Springsteen and Dylan created greater impact than the band's own music,' but there was 'nothing wrong in using other people's songs for your own ends', and it was 'a refreshing change to find that modesty in artists of such maturity and expertise'.

Now they had a chart album as well as a single, all the dates sold out. The next three weeks were taken up with eight gigs in America, the last being at Kent State University, Ohio, on 6 November. After one show at Youngstown in October, Tom Doyle remarked in his review in *Beaver County Times* that Manfred had just returned with 'one of the best mature rock albums of the year' and proved beyond doubt that what he had just seen was 'a completely new group ready to tackle the competition of the seventies'. *The Roaring Silence* looked set to become their biggest record to date, and 'if Springsteen could only do his own material as well as other people do, then he might someday be a success himself'.

After a short break, they played three dates in Sweden in the first week of December, followed by three in the second half of the month in England and Wales, finishing up with their first major headlining appearance in London at the New Victoria Theatre. It was also the occasion on which they premiered a song that would become one of the jewels in their crown, 'Davy's on the Road Again', which they dedicated onstage to their new guitarist.

'I would seek to have the band be very successful,' Manfred admitted to Hugh Fielder in *Sounds* towards the end of the year, and at last, he had steered the band to solid success, not just with a solitary top 10 single, but also achieved respectability with a more faithful fan base in the album charts.

Right: *The Roaring Silence.*
The group's only top ten
album in the US and UK,
and a US gold album, 1976.
(Creature Music)

Left: *The Roaring Silence.* 'Blinded by
the Light' was a US number one and
UK number six, though 'Questions'
never charted, 1976. *(Creature
Music)*

Below: The group with new members
Chris Thompson (vocals, guitar) and
Dave Flett (lead guitar) on left, 1976.

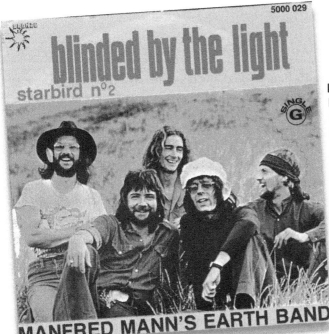

5000 029

blinded by the light
starbird n°2

SINGLE G

MANFRED MANN'S EARTH BAND

Left: 'Blinded by the Light', Portuguese single picture sleeve. 'Deuce' or 'douche'? Whatever, it proved their international breakthrough hit in 1976.

Above: The group basking in major worldwide success, at last, in 1976.

1977-78

Manfred Mann's Earth Band would always remember 1977 as the year they achieved a chart-topper in America, something the keyboard player had done only once before, with 'Do Wah Diddy Diddy'. After a series of dates in Germany and Switzerland during January, they went to America for a tour that lasted from February to the beginning of April. It coincided with 'Blinded by the Light' climbing to the coveted No. 1 position for one week, something Bruce Springsteen never achieved during a lengthy career with any of his own singles on either side of the Atlantic.

Chris Slade said that the whole group were amazed by the news. Someone from Warner Bros told him that he knew the record was a hit as soon as he heard it. 'That's funny, because we didn't,' was his reply. 'We didn't have a clue. It was a complete shock.' The album also stayed in the American charts for 37 weeks, having initially peaked at number 117 and started dropping before being revived by the success of the single, climbing to number 10 (the same position as in Britain).

Warner Bros were anxious to strike while the iron was hot, and follow up a chart-topping single in America with another relatively commercial track. As they did not hear one on *The Roaring Silence*, they asked for a re-recording of 'Spirit in the Night', or rather for Chris Thompson to add his voice to the backing track, just leaving Mick Rogers' vocal backing without the lead. They were touring a snow-covered America at the time, but Chris duly obliged, taking the group's sound engineer Mick Williams with him. One night in March 1977, while on the road in St Louis, Missouri, they drove 50 miles to the studio, recorded the new vocal, did a quick mix, and jumped back in the car, driving as fast as conditions would allow so they could be back at the hotel in time for dinner. On returning and getting out of the car, Mick was horrified when he couldn't find the large flat box in which he had safely put the tape. Then he remembered he had left it on the roof outside the studio and forgot to place it inside. Much to their relief, it was still on the roof, covered in snow. That was one near-disaster they kept a closely guarded secret for many years.

The winter weather during part of their American tour in early 1977 had another beneficial result. After their warm-up shows (a perhaps ironic turn of phrase), they found themselves snowed in at a club in Boulder, Colorado, and could not get out for a week. As the next few shows had to be postponed, Manfred made a deal with the club owner, allowing them to use the facility so they could rehearse songs for the forthcoming album every day, and they had recording equipment set up so they could gauge the progress of the new material. Chris Thompson recalled he had been looking forward to a few days of tobogganing and throwing snowballs at each other instead, 'but it was not to be'.

The result was issued as a follow-up that spring and gave the group an American Top 40 hit. (A few advance promotional copies escaped with the one-word title 'Spirit', corrected as soon as the mistake was realised.) Bronze Records followed suit in Britain during the summer, again adhering to the title 'Spirits in the Night', but to no significant airplay and zero chart success. Meanwhile, Vertigo sought to cash in on their newfound success with a compilation of earlier material, *1971–1973*, with sleeve notes by Mick Rogers. Released only in Britain and Germany, it attracted little attention, although the ten-track selection did at least allow fans to obtain an album including 'Joybringer', which had never been on LP in Britain. It never subsequently appeared on CD.

Colin Pattenden left in the spring, his last gig with the group being the final date of their American tour at Baltimore on 3 April. His replacement was initially to be Mark Clarke, who had previously played bass guitar with Uriah Heep, Colosseum and Tempest. All of them having been on the Bronze label, he had close connections with Gerry Bron, who told him one day that Manfred had regularly asked about him and would like a meeting. As a result, they played several songs together, and Manfred seemed impressed. However, it never progressed any further. The one who landed the job would be Pat King, a Scottish bass guitarist who had been a member of Lulu's backing group The Luvvers, and then The Tremors, whose main claim to fame was including future Rockpile guitarist Billy Bremner in their line-up. He was subsequently a member of Shanghai with Mick Green, and also as a session musician for Cat Stevens, Billy Ocean, The Nolans and The Dooleys, among others. In 1971 he had been a member of progressive band Trifle, whose only album that year had included their version of 'One Way Glass'.

After a few weeks' rehearsal, the new line-up played their first dates in Holland, Sweden and Germany in May and June. The opening one and the highlight among these was the Pinkpop Festival at Limburg in the Netherlands on 30 May, headlined by The Kinks and also featuring Nils Lofgren, Tom Petty and the Heartbreakers and Golden Earring. A seven-song set included 'The Road to Babylon', 'Spirits in the Night', 'Blinded by the Light', 'Father of Day, Father of Night', and, as ever, concluded with 'Mighty Quinn'. In August, they played what would be their last shows of the year, two major German festivals at Berlin and Esslingen in August with Uriah Heep and the briefly re-formed Small Faces also on the bill.

Although there were fewer gigs for them than in previous years, the group were kept busy in other directions. A new album was in production while Chris Thompson was invited by producer Jeff Wayne to add vocals to 'Thunder Child', a track on the concept double album *The War of the Worlds*, which on its release in 1978 would rarely be far from the British album charts for the best part of six years. He also guested on Elton John's *A Single Man* album and joined Elton and his band on tour to promote the album. He also formed a part-time group, Filthy McNasty, which had a residency for several months over 1977–78 at the Bridge House, Canning Town, London. The line-up also included vocalist Stevie Lange, former Back Street Crawler guitarist Geoff Whitehorn, from time to time Nicky Hopkins, the sessions king of the keyboards, and American harmonica player Huey Lewis. They were more of a soul pub band, being, in Stevie's words 'a cross between Ike and Tina Turner and Boston', with a repertoire including the Janis Joplin favourite 'Move Over', and as one of the high points of their set, a Chris-Stevie duet on The Temptations' 'I Can't Get Next to You'. Chris enjoyed the gigs three nights a week as the Earth Band were off the road, and he saw it as a good way of keeping his voice in shape and having fun at the same time – and above all, he hated being idle. They committed three tracks to vinyl on *A Week at the Bridge*, issued as a one-off by the pub on its Bridge House label in 1978, a compilation featuring other acts who played there regularly, on a package consisting of an LP and a 12" single.

Meanwhile, Manfred found employment of a different kind. In 1977 he temporarily joined the world of academia, being co-opted as a Fellow to the University of London Goldsmith College, where he lectured on music theory to students.

For many people, the year would be remembered as the year that punk rock turned the British music scene upside down – or did it? Manfred never deviated from his view that punk was partly a journalist's dream. It might be full of attitude, but there was no concealing the fact that some of the music was simply bad. He refused to believe that the end of the world was nigh. To Chris Welch, he conceded that he had been around a long time, long enough to be part of the old order, but he was not still playing the same music as he had a few years before. 'It's all changing, and we're playing music.' Musical anarchy had its place, but it was not going to overthrow 'the old order' or consign it to oblivion overnight, and unlike some of his contemporaries in the music world, he refused to regard it as any kind of threat. 'I actually don't think a new order ever comes. It's just a vague conglomeration of things, isn't it? So the Sex Pistols go overboard to be revolting? That's cool. So did Kiss. Are Kiss punk rock? Yeah? Well that's cool, if it's good.'

Significantly, it was also the time that ELP, Yes, Genesis and ELO could be found regularly competing with The Clash, The Sex Pistols and The Stranglers (thanks to Dave Greenfield's distinctive keyboard-playing, perhaps the only act most of the older musicians really liked) in the singles and albums charts. Punk rock might have been a reaction against a music scene that some thought was becoming old and staid, but others were prescient enough to see it as evolution. There was evidently room for everyone and everything.

With regard to Kiss, who had been on the same bill as them for several American dates in 1974, Manfred was asked if it annoyed him that they needed to use make-up and gimmicks as opposed to concentrating exclusively on the music. It didn't bother him at all. Kiss, he said, were very imaginative with their make-up, clothes and stage act. 'The main thing is that when you do something, you do it well, and these people obviously do.' Although the Earth Band had never subscribed to the idea of dressing up in outrageous or striking costumes in concert, they paid great attention to lighting and presentation. Chris Thompson was impressed to discover that Manfred had a car wing mirror fitted onto his Moog, so he could keep a careful eye on the lights behind and above the group while they were playing.

A trailer for the forthcoming album, 'California', was released as a single in Britain in November. Written by Sue Vickers, then wife of Mike, a member of the old group in the early 1960s, it received generous airplay on Radio 1, becoming a record of the week on the Tony Blackburn mid-morning show, and a new release spot on *Top of the Pops*. Chris thought it would be amusing to dress up for their appearance on the programme with a big scarf and woolly hat. Unfortunately for him, there was an equipment malfunction while the show was being recorded. He had to stay onstage under the bright lights for half an hour, sweating profusely, while Billy Idol of Generation X, also on the programme that week and in the studio, was sneering at him. Sadly for all their efforts, although singles sales were buoyant at the time in Britain, it failed to progress beyond the Top 50 breakers.

Watch (1978)

Personnel:
Manfred Mann: keyboards, backing vocals
Chris Hamlet Thompson: vocals, guitar
Dave Flett: lead and acoustic guitars
Pat King: bass guitar, backing vocals
Chris Slade: drums, percussion
Additional musicians:
Doreen Chanter, Irene Chanter, Stevie Lange, Victy Silva, Kim Goddy: backing vocals
Producer: Manfred Mann and Earth Band
Studio: The Workhouse, Old Kent Road, London
Release date: February 1978
Chart placings: UK: 33; US: 83
Running time: 39:26
Label: Bronze (UK), Warner Bros (US)
Side One: 1. Circles (Alan Mark) 2. Drowning on Dry Land/Fish Soup (Chris Slade, Dave Flett, Manfred Mann) 3. Chicago Institute (Peter Thomas, Manfred Mann, Dave Flett) 4. California (Sue Vickers)
Side Two: 5. Davy's on the Road Again (live) (John Simon) 6, Martha's Madman (Lane Tietgen) 7. Mighty Quinn (live) (Bob Dylan)
Bonus tracks: Cohesion (1998)
8. California (single edit) (Sue Vickers) 9. Davy's on the Road Again (single edit) (John Simon, Robbie Robertson) 10. Bouillabaisse (single edit) (Dave Flett, Manfred Mann) 11. Mighty Quinn (single edit) (Bob Dylan)

'Circles', the opening track, is a haunting, dramatic number with plenty of light and shade. Ethereal organ paves the way for Chris's vocals on a song that builds to a bombastic break with keyboard effects sounding like a heavy strings section and a soaring guitar solo from Dave, before it fades back into a subdued final vocal section. At times it sounds a little reminiscent of Argent, or seems to reference mid-1970s ELO or Kansas. As for the lyrics, these are open to varying interpretations, but it is generally agreed that the theme is basically one of solitude, despair and loneliness, with fans and listeners not slow to voice their thoughts online in the internet age. 'Going round in circles, directions all messed up ... I'm a clown without a circus, there's no-one to see my act.' Is it about somebody who has just broken up after a relationship, someone going mad, or as has been suggested, a pilot trying to land but has somehow lost control of his plane?

'Drowning on Dry Land / Fish Soup' is a track made up of two parts, as the title indicates. The first two minutes are relatively laid-back, the song following a similar downbeat theme to that of the preceding track – an isolated figure who sits in a silent room, with the walls around him screaming, standing between light and dark. The mood is reinforced by a chorus indicating helplessness, of 'drowning on dry land, vast adrift on an empty sea'. Musically, it is taken at a slow pace, with acoustic guitar and dreamy keyboards. Two minutes in, an instrumental section follows as the pace quickens with some snappy electric guitar chords, a more forceful rhythm on the drums and soaring keyboard theme. Nearly another two minutes later, it slows down again, with a reprise of the vocal section repeating the chorus lines, accompanied by spacey synth work.

'Chicago Institute' is a mid-tempo piece that briefly relaxes the pace for about 30 seconds halfway through. An insistent guitar riff with colourful keyboards, plus stomping drums and bass to match, at times, it almost threatens to go into a disco rhythm, something which few acts escaped completely in the late 1970s. As for the subject matter of the lyrics, they are probably the most enigmatic on the whole record. Initially, it was supposed to be about a dubious mental institution, with its opening lines, 'There's an institute in Chicago with a room full of machines, And they live this side of the sunrise and burn away your dreams.' Some years later, journalist Don Jacobson of Beachwood Reporter looked at a few songs that dwelt on the writers' love-hate relationship with Chicago. He called it 'basically a paranoid rant about how computers literally have our numbers … a stroll down Orwell Lane – about how Big Brother controls our meaningless, numbered lives from the cradle to the grave, and about how only rebellious individualism can save our basic humanity'. Big Brother, he added, was evidently based in Chicago.

A peaceful few seconds led by acoustic guitar open 'California', the full-length version of the album's first single, characterised above all by Chris's vocal, which for the most part is pitched quite high. The falsetto singing had been Pat's idea, partly as what he called 'a back-handed compliment to the Beach Boys'. Nevertheless, Chris said later that he hated the song as he thought it was far too sweet and pretty for an Earth Band number. Despite the sunny, upbeat mood, it is quite a plaintive, sombre lyric, sung from the point of view of one who wants to know how his partner is doing far away in California, 'now that you've made the grade, is there a chance you'd think of me?' One day, he assures her, he will make it out there himself to see if it is what it really seems, as he has been there so many times before, 'but only in my dreams'. For the most part, it is a gentle, relaxed song, with only a guitar break later on coming upfront to add a little extra fire.

'California' may have been not quite attention-grabbing enough to seize the ear of singles buyers, but an absolute earworm on side two eventually did. 'Davy's on the Road Again' had been written about eight years earlier by John Simon, whose work was already known to Manfred Mann as he had written and previously recorded 'My Name is Jack', a hit in 1968 for the old band. Although he recorded and released a few albums in his own right, he was better known as a producer for Leonard Cohen and The Band, of whom he was sometimes known as 'the sixth member', playing keyboards and horns on their second album. 'Davy's on the Road Again' is credited on *Watch*, and elsewhere as being co-written with Robbie Robertson, although a post on YouTube by John's son asserts that the song was entirely his father's work. The original version had appeared on an album he issued in 1971 and caught the attention of Manfred, who owned a copy of the song and several of his other tracks on tape for some years, and was particularly drawn to that one. There are some classical overtones in the melody, with a resemblance between the verse and a section from 'By the River', the second movement from *Florida Suite*, composed by Frederick Delius in 1887. All the different nuances in Delius's melody and arrangement, including the minor and major chords, are clearly discernible in John's recording, which the Earth Band follow faithfully.

The group had rearranged it and included it in their stage act for over a year and advised him that they really ought to record it, but he was unsure of its potential. Eventually, he was persuaded, and he realised that it had a certain charm because of the way it started as a ballad and then picked up with the irresistible boogie shuffle that Status Quo had perfected so spectacularly during the last few years. A few elaborate crossfades showed him that it could work. They gave it an intro with shimmering organ and vocal, then gradually brought in the bass guitar, added drums a few seconds later, and by developing it with a couple of three-note hooks on synth and then blazing guitar solo, turned it into a really special piece of work. Some note-bending on the synths and a brief passage where everything cut away except the lead vocal on the last verse, proved the icing on the cake. The infectious chorus rapidly made it a live favourite in Britain and Europe, and it would regularly bring audiences to their feet as they joined in. Pat's bass playing is particularly effective, and he was thoroughly flattered when he later met a professor of music from Trondheim in a bar there once, they got chatting, and he said that Pat's bass on that particular track was one of his favourite pieces to listen to.

'Martha's Madman' is also another fairly instant song that would also remain a live favourite for a long time. Again, insistent bass guitar underpins the rest of the instruments with an infectious song on top that eventually goes into overdrive as guitar and Moog share out the honours on the solo.

Finally came the song they had never been able to leave behind onstage, six and a half minutes of 'Mighty Quinn', with the more powerful, almost heavy rock rearrangement that they had given it ever since they had got together at the start of the decade. This live version begins with quiet organ and subdued guitar, and the audience's roar of recognition. Two minutes in comes a guitar and synth break, which speeds up another couple of minutes after that. Throughout the song sections, the guitar packs a strong punch between the lines, and for the last 30 seconds, until fading out the audience are clapping along and singing their hearts out. Although some fans considered it rather redundant, others appreciated being able to compare the more up-to-date take after having been familiar with the 1968 version for so long. Chris Thompson said their performance of the song always got the audience going and that it was 'a thing with Manfred' to spot the person in the audience not singing along. 'Perhaps he should have been concentrating on other things!'

A striking sleeve design for the album was produced by Michael Sanz as two separate oil paintings on canvases, both 60 x 60 cm. The figure of the man on the runway was suggested by the group's Swedish tour manager Thomas Johansson, who had seen it in an advertisement over there and pointed it out when they arrived in Stockholm for some dates.

Watch is, in retrospect, seen as the album that made Manfred Mann's Earth Band more of a conventional, more commercial pop-rock group. The more ambitiously constructed epics, plus the lengthy eight-minute jams and improvisations, were becoming a thing of the past, with more potential singles to be heard. It was a change that left fans with mixed feelings. Some felt that they were leaving their prog rock principles behind, while others applauded them for moving on from a genre that had been right for the early 1970s but was becoming passé, particularly in the light of the shake-up that punk and new wave had given the British music scene in the last couple of years.

There were still some criticisms of the almost total lack of self-penned material, to which Manfred answered with modesty that he was very proud of the fact. 'If you can write great songs, put them on the album,' he insisted. 'We pride ourselves on being flexible, on being able to take the best material at our disposal without worrying who wrote it. In a nutshell, we don't think we write good enough songs.'

In March, shortly after the album was released, the group went to Europe for a month of touring, mostly in Germany, where their dedicated following always assured them of an enthusiastic reception. Pat particularly treasured his memory of playing a German festival at around this time when they took to the stage as it was pouring with rain. As they began playing, the sun suddenly came out, the crowd went wild, and after that, they could do no wrong.

April was taken up with dates in England prior to an appearance in America in June. A new remade, remodelled 'Mighty Quinn', a new version that started with about 15 seconds of the live version half the album length, then edited into a new studio recording, had been chosen as the second single in Britain – to commemorate the tenth anniversary of the chart-topping studio version. Ads in the music press assured buyers that 'You'll not hear nothing like the new "Mighty Quinn"'. Although the group were proud of their new version, none of them really liked the idea of putting it out as a single. The original version was still fairly fresh in everyone's memory and had long been a regularly aired golden oldie on the radio, and they thought it was a totally retrograde step. Yet Manfred had little choice but to bow to record company and managerial pressure. It did not follow 'California' on to daytime radio, so how much Bronze Records' scheme of using it to promote the new album had the right effect is anyone's guess.

During March, the 'Watch' tour found them taking to the road and playing to ever-faithful audiences in Germany, Scandinavia and Switzerland. Manfred told *NME* that he was genuinely surprised by how successful the group were proving on the continent at this time.

Having gone through a period of total failure, I find it quite incredible what is happening in Europe. I'm doing so much better than in the mid-sixties when we were having hit singles all the time. When I think back to the sixties and having achieved household status – if that's an achievement – and now I'm playing modern music in 1978 – the argument over just how modern it is and whether it's just another boring old fart doing the rounds is ultimately a small one; the fact is that young people find it modern – it's quite incredible.

In April, they played several shows in England and Scotland, followed by one more gig that year, in June, at New Jersey. A performance at the Rainbow, London, brought forth an almost ecstatic review in *The Times*, 14 April 1978, from Robert Shelton, who noted that their métier was:

A skilful mix of the abstract, the surreal and the real ... always sophisticated yet avoids the temptation to ride above the head of the audience. The Earth Band tends, in the best tradition of popular music, to animate while it elevates ... Mann is, perhaps by virtue of his jazz background, a technician who has not forgotten about the necessity of pulse and swinging, and constant communication. Cerebral rock that swings, churns, piques, unsettles inevitably, excites, is a rare mixture these days ... The energy, urgency and technical brilliance were astounding.

Chris Thompson was gradually discovering for himself that audiences were more appreciative and less reserved in some countries than others. They all considered themselves lucky to have been successful in Germany and toured so much there because the German people 'really stand beside you as an artist'. Like the Americans, 'they really know how to do a concert and how to be a concert audience. The British are a bit more kind of "Show us exactly what you have, Mr Thompson, and we'll clap if we think it's fantastic" – well, not all of them, but a lot of them are, whereas the German audiences get there and they're really up for a great time.'

Although they had found a new level of success in Britain during the last two or three years, they found it hard not to feel a measure of disdain for some sections of the media in their own country and their obsession with street credibility. Many other groups who had been around for a similar length of time had had to put up with similar treatment. But at the end of the day, their steady level of record success – selling out concerts and enjoying some level of consistent success in the singles and albums charts from which they had been largely absent in the earlier years of the decade – spoke for itself. 'There was a kind of democracy about the rock business', an element of free choice and following his own inclinations that he could enjoy, he told *Sounds*.

I'm a real capitalist about the music business; it's so much better to let people decide on the basis of their own ears than on cultural grounds. I don't want a committee of people deciding what's right, good or fashionable. And I certainly can't base my career on appealing to the hip journalists who are raving over the latest fashions.

Although the live 'Mighty Quinn' had slipped by virtually unnoticed, their luck changed for the better when an edited 'Davy's on the Road Again' hit the shops at the end of April. Shortened by over two minutes through omission of the guitar solo near the start and the audience singalong section close to the end, given a discreet fade-out, and with added female vocals, it restored them to British top 10 favour after the previous singles had failed to register. It proved arguably the most infectious three-and-a-half minutes of music that they would ever commit to vinyl. Chris Thompson knew they were on to a winner, saying he was so happy that they had recorded 'a good old-fashioned rock 'n' roll shuffle', something they did all too rarely. John Peel, who had become Radio 1's resident champion of punk rock and dismissed 'California' as utterly bland, gave it his seal of approval, while Dave Lee Travis chose it as his record of the week on the same station's breakfast show (the group's third single to be granted such an accolade in less than two years), and it took them back to number 6 that summer. The B-side, 'Bouillabaisse', as most people had worked out for themselves, was 'Fish Soup', edited as the second part (or helping, one might say) of the album's second track.

Ironically, despite their American success during the previous two years, Warner Bros issued both 'California' and 'Davy's on the Road Again' to zero chart action, and the album managed only six weeks in the listings. In Britain, the album had been slow to take off, selling in insufficient numbers to make the chart until after the tour was over and only once the single was in the Top 10. German buyers proved as faithful as ever, and there it became not only their most successful album ever but also the third biggest-selling album of the year, after the unstoppable *Saturday Night Fever* and *Grease* soundtracks.

The full second side of *Watch* would remain a staple part of the group's live set for some time to come. It was appropriate as the album had been split into a studio side (the first) and a live one. Manfred told *Beat Magazine* that he preferred the studio one as it was gentler 'with a nice flowing vibe about it', while the other was more exciting and upfront. In the same interview, Chris Thompson added that the trio of live songs was more representative of them for a change. 'The other albums are all much gentler than the band really is. The band is a loud, energetic outfit – you don't get this from the records.' Manfred had resisted the urge, or the advice of others, to put in-concert material on their albums on the grounds that 'the live tapes sounded pretty crappy'. The ideal compromise, he then realised, was to take a good quality in-concert performance on tape and hone it to perfection in the studio.

In August 1978, they returned to the studios to begin work on the next album. However, the constant workload, or treadmill, of touring and studio work was taking its toll, and the atmosphere in the group had deteriorated. During the tour, Manfred had been watching them carefully and was disheartened by the arguments and fighting that were going on offstage, not involving him, but between other members of the group. He thought it was all quite unnecessary, and ironic. During the early 1970s, the band had been struggling, at times 'almost a complete failure'. Now they were playing to audiences of several thousand every night, and instead of thinking 'this is a bloody miracle', they were bickering among themselves and getting fed up with each other. There was only one thing for it – to disband and start again. Chris Slade and Dave Flett accordingly left and recording sessions for the new songs were placed on hold while Manfred, Chris Thompson and Pat King considered their position, prior to breaking in a new line-up.

For a short time, there was the feeling that Manfred was intending to retire from the active music scene. Chris Slade and Colin Pattenden asked him whether it would be in order for them to form a new Earth Band, keep the name and recruit additional musicians. As Manfred raised no objections to the idea, they recruited Chris West, a guitarist who'd previously collaborated with Steve Winwood and Stomu Yamashta, Peter Cox, a young vocalist who would later enjoy his greatest success with Go West, and Roy Shipston, who had played in prog rock band Rococo alongside future Judie Tzuke Band, Dexys Midnight Runners and Status Quo bass guitarist John 'Rhino' Edwards. After rehearsals and warm-up gigs, they toured England, Germany and Holland as support to The Scorpions, playing Earth Band material alongside songs written mostly by Chris West and Peter Cox.

Following an injunction from Bronze Records, ordering them to cease and desist from working as Earth Band, Chris suggested that they become Terra Nova ('new earth'), thus maintaining a connection with the old name. Otherwise, it was business as usual for them and they recorded an album at Rock City Studios, Shepperton (which Chris Slade and Colin both co-managed for a while), released in 1980 on the Swiss label BB Records. After being unable to get sufficient interest in any other markets, they then disbanded, although Roy Shipston maintained an Earth Band connection when he subsequently worked with a band later formed by their then-current vocalist, Chris Thompson and the Islands.

Pat King had long been familiar with the Sunday jam sessions at the Half Moon, Herne Hill, a well-known music haunt where members of Thin Lizzy and the Jeff Beck Band hung out and played regularly. As he knew several of the regular players, he advised Manfred to go there and check out Steve Waller, a guitarist and singer who had been a member of British soul-funk outfit Gonzalez, had played on their recent hit 'Haven't Stopped Dancing Yet', and was often to be seen performing as part of the house band. Manfred was duly impressed and one audition was enough to secure his place in the new line-up. Steve had initially been in two minds about joining, after having told a friend – perhaps tongue-in-cheek – that he thought Manfred Mann was just a cabaret act, before he realised this was clearly not the case.

Meanwhile, the vacant drum stool was filled by Geoff Britton, whose previous bands had included Paul McCartney's Wings, Wild Angels and East of Eden, who had once supported Manfred Mann Chapter Three on tour. Both new members gelled at once, and the album was almost completed by the end of the year.

Right: *Watch*. The album that many fans felt saw the group moving away from progressive rock into more commercial pastures, 1978. *(Creature Music)*

Left: The group after Pat King (bass) on the right had replaced Colin Pattenden, in 1978.

Right: Chris Thompson and Manfred Mann, 1978.

Left: Chris Thompson, who also played in part-time pub band Filthy McNasty and guested on Jeff Wayne's *War of the Worlds.*

Right: The programme for the UK and European tour, March and April 1978. *Watch* became their most successful album in Germany, reaching number three.

Manfred Mann's
Earth Band
WATCH
European & UK Tour 78

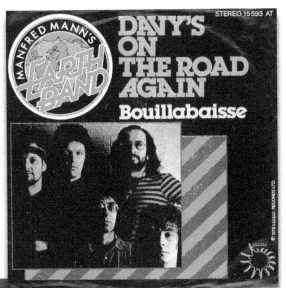

Right: 'Davy's on the Road Again', German single picture sleeve. It went top 30 in Germany, but top ten in Britain and Ireland, in 1978.

Left: The group in 1979, with Steve Waller (guitar, vocals) and John Lingwood (drums) on the left.

Right: *Angel Station.* The sleeve design echoes the geometrical perspectives of Swiss artist M.C. Escher. *(Creature Music)*

Left and below: The group promoting 'Davy's on the Road Again' on BBC's *Top of the Pops,* May 1978.

PAT KING BASS & STEVE WALLER LEAD

picato

Buy The only strings they'll play

picato
STRINGS

Sound Magic in The Earthband

Available from your dealer now

General Music Strings, Treforest, Mid-Glamorgan.

Left: Pat King and Steve Waller, endorsing Picato guitar and bass guitar strings.

1979

At the start of 1979, the new line-up could look forward to several months of dates across Europe and Britain. The new album was completed in January, but with a greater reliance on outside assistance than previously. To augment the new line-up in the studio came Jimme O'Neill of Fingerprintz on rhythm guitar, Dyan Birch, formerly of Arrival and Kokomo, and Stevie Lange both on backing vocals, Graham Preskett on violin, and for once an outside producer, Anthony Moore, formerly of Henry Cow and Slapp Happy, who also contributed additional guitar and sequencer parts. Manfred was credited as 'executive producer', evidently happy to allow someone else with his finger more on the pulse to take the proverbial driving seat.

As a taster for the album, 'You Angel You' preceded it as a single in February. A Bob Dylan number from the 1973 album *Planet Waves*, it was far and away the most commercial of his songs that the Earth Band had yet covered, with an instantly recognisable hook in the chorus. 'Manfred's bank balance is a bit low, so here comes another Bob Dylan song,' quipped *NME* at the head of its review. Modest airtime helped to send it to No. 54 in the British chart, and the album followed a month later.

Angel Station (1979)

Personnel:
Manfred Mann: keyboards, vocals (Resurrection, bridge of Don't Kill it Carol)
Chris Thompson: vocals (chorus of Don't Kill It Carol, You Angel You, Hollywood Town, 'Belle' of the Earth, You Are – I Am, Waiting for the Rain), guitar
Steve Waller: guitar (verse of Don't Kill it Carol, You Angel You, 'Belle' of the Earth, Angels at My Gate, You Are – I Am), vocals
Pat King: bass guitar
Geoff Britton: drums, alto saxophone
Additional musicians:
Anthony Moore: guitar, sequencer, synthesiser
Jimme O'Neill: rhythm guitar, arrangements
Graham Preskett: violin (Waiting for the Rain)
Dyan Birch, Anne Kelly: backing vocals
John Potter: choral arrangements

Producer: Anthony Moore
Studio: The Workhouse, Old Kent Road, London, Dunowen (Noel Redding's House), Clonakilty, County Cork
Release date: March 1979
Chart placings: UK: 30; US: 144
Running time: 38:47
Label: Bronze (UK), Warner Bros (US)
Side One: 1. Don't Kill it Carol (Mike Heron) 2. You Angel You (Bob Dylan)
3. Hollywood Town (Harriet Schock) 4. 'Belle' of the Earth (Manfred Mann)
5. Platform End (Manfred Mann, Geoff Britton, Pat King, Steve Waller, Chris Thompson, Jimme O'Neill)
Side Two: 6. Angels at my Gate (Manfred Mann, Hirth Martinez, Jimme O'Neill) 7. You Are – I Am (Manfred Mann) 8. Waiting for the Rain (Billy Falcon)
9. Resurrection (Manfred Mann)
Bonus tracks: Cohesion (1998)
10. Don't Kill it Carol (single version) (Mike Heron) 11. You Angel You (single version) (Bob Dylan)

The full versions of both tracks that would also appear as singles launch the album. 'Don't Kill it Carol', another song from the pen of Mike Heron, has a gentle environmental theme – 'This wild rose that I hold in my hand, it could grow to be so strong … Oh Carol, oh, won't you let this flower grow'. New guitarist Steve Waller contributes an interesting section on vocoder in the lower range for the verses that contrasts well with Chris Thompson's singing in a higher pitch on the chorus. It was a particular favourite of Pat, who loved it, both as a recording and on live shows, for its strong riff, melody and the solo, which, he said, 'started out as very fragmented and then picked up in intensity before returning to the melody, and a very balanced juxtaposition of lead vocals'. The rhythm shows a subtle text in the direction of disco – this was 1979, after all – and there are hints of an ELO sound in some cello-like flourishes on the keyboard.

Watch had been unique among the group's 1970s catalogue in that it didn't feature any Bob Dylan or Bruce Springsteen numbers. This time they made up for it, and handsomely too. Although they take no real significant liberties with the original song from Dylan's 1973 album *Planet Waves*, their version of 'You Angel You' immediately demonstrates how they managed to bend it slightly to bring out the catchiness of the melody, as well as throwing in one or two neat little curves from the keys and drums on the instrumental break.

Pat made an unusual contribution to the track, and in fact, the whole record. He had recently watched *Close Encounters of the Third Kind* and was fascinated by the sounds from the spaceship. Heavily influenced by these, he came up with a sequence of six notes that were used in the intro of the song and then played at varying speeds through a sequencer later in the track. The same notes were then used in the arrangement of most of the other songs on the album.

Most of the Earth Band's previous forays into the Zimmermann songbook from 1971 onwards had really sounded more like album tracks and suggested Manfred might have lost his mojo when it came to turning them into something chart-friendly as he had done in earlier years. But more than anything else since his days at the keyboards behind Paul Jones and Michael d'Abo, in its shortened form this has 'hit single' written all over it. (The modest, even unnecessary, edit removes only about 20 seconds of the intro from the album version.) Next to 'Davy's on the Road Again', it was arguably the most commercial number they had yet recorded. In *Melody Maker*, Chris Welch singled it out as 'one of the outstanding performances on this vibrant, cleverly wrought album' and as proof that Manfred has 'an alchemist's touch'.

It was one of the first songs they tried out in which Chris and Steve combined their vocals. At first, Chris disliked the idea of their sharing the singing, but after they had tried it, he had to admit that Manfred had used the combination of both voices to make a very strong album. Onstage it rapidly became a favourite, expanded to over eight minutes with additional keyboard wizardry from Manfred and slide guitar solo from Steve.

'Hollywood Town', by Harriet Schock, an American singer-songwriter whose songs were covered mostly by American artists, has a reflective, almost sinister lyric about the tawdriness of the city where 'the lost and found come to find their way', the emptiness beneath the glossy image. A heavy beat on the drums, again not far from disco, and a screaming solo from the synths on the break give it a strong late 1970s feel.

Of the five original numbers on the album, '"Belle" of the Earth' is the first of three credited solely to Manfred, who may have taken the comments to heart after the preponderance of cover versions on the previous album. Like the previous song, in the introspective lyrics, there are echoes of the emptiness of life in a large city – London this time, possibly – where the subway lies ahead, but there's no music to be heard, and 'there's something wrong in this town'. It is clearly a tale of somebody feeling isolated, and perhaps drawing on that mood for artistic inspiration. Synth-pop sounds provide the intro with an ethereal synth as what starts off as a slow, almost bluesy number and then gradually gathers momentum, again with that almost but not quite disco punch on the drums. The keyboards provide most of the backing, with guitar little in evidence, while the instrumental break towards the fade-out is quite short. Had they recorded this earlier in the decade, it would doubtless have developed into a lengthy, improvisational epic. But Manfred had left that behind them, and it is all wrapped up in less than three minutes.

Even briefer is the closest the album gets to an instrumental, 'Platform End'. A 90-second interlude with just a few seconds of indecipherable vocal before the fade, this run-of-the-mill track is no more than a chance for both guitars and keyboards to pit themselves against each other, plus all five members and Jimme O'Neill to share joint writing credits. Some years later, the title would live on as also the name of Manfred Mann's Earth Band's fanzine, and, subsequently, in the internet age, the official website.

'Angels at my Gate' is as contemporary as they come, not far removed from the style that the likes of Gary Numan, Kraftwerk and even early Human League were about to bring to the masses. This is a dark, murky number, with what sounds like mid-eastern-influenced keyboards and electronic drumming. The lyrics tell of a world of clowns and gamblers with fingers on the dial as the lucky wheel goes round, jokers laughing as the stakes get higher, while the gambler and the clown without a safety net balance unsteadily on a wire. Steve's voice-box guitar provides some spark to an otherwise quite laid-back number with its other-worldly atmosphere. Some have remarked in retrospect that it could have had an influence on Peter Gabriel, not least his next major hit 'Games Without Frontiers' the following year. Chris was very impressed with the way in which Manfred had mixed the work of both vocalists together, Steve in the verses while he sang the choruses.

Cleverly bridging a gap between their old style and the new, 'You Are – I Am' continues a soft-focused electro-pop style in the first half. Manfred subtly references two of the earlier albums in his lyric:

You are the time between solar fire and the silence;
You are the last chord in the symphony of the lost.
You are the sign between the high road and the low road,
You are the pen in the moving hand of time.'

Then the more familiar Moog stylings of yore and a few touches of lead guitar take centre stage. A review by Chris Welch suggested that it was reminiscent of some of The Beatles' later, more experimental work. It received a revival of sorts in 2010 when Kanye West featured a sample in 'So Appalled' on his album *My Beautiful Dark Twisted Fantasy*, Manfred and Kanye, thus being two of the nine people to get a joint writing credit on the track. What goes around comes around, and Manfred subsequently returned the favour four years later when he added new keyboards to 'So Appalled', with an added chorus from Caitlyn Scarlett, on his album *Lone Arranger*.

'Waiting for the Rain' is undoubtedly the prettiest song on the album, if not indeed on any of the group's 1970s albums. Pure love songs are not generally high on the agenda of the average prog rock act, but this haunting number written by American songwriter Billy Falcon is a touching piece written to his wife, someone who deserves the sunshine and not the rain: 'you deserve the rainbow, you've had enough pain'. Chris Thompson gives a marvellous emotional performance to a lyric that tugs at the heartstrings. Graham Preskett's violins add to the mood of poignancy, with a stirring trumpet voluntary on synth from the main man.

Finally, 'Resurrection' is a jaunty song that verges on music hall territory. Misunderstood at the time, it was thought to be a satire on the second coming of Christ. A closer examination of the lyrics, all Manfred's own work, reveal that it is a commentary on how an unscrupulous businessman could seek to exploit that second coming to financial advantage via merchandising. 'We'll sell them Jesus hats, Jesus socks, Jesus coats, We'll sue the Pope, Jesus shoes, Jesus dirty books too, I wonder what will Billy Graham do.' Opening with angelic choral vocals and then breaking out into a jaunty, slightly music-hall setting, It could almost have come from the pen of the man who wrote the Earth Band's first single, Randy Newman, who later revealed a gift for poking fun at aspects of the world around him. Towards the end, a close listen will reveal the sound of someone shouting 'any old iron', followed by laughter. Fearing objections from the Bible Belt and the threat of radio station bans in America, Warner Bros discreetly omitted the lyrics from the inner sleeve.

The album was originally going to be named *Choice*, with a sleeve design showing a graph that buyers could colour in any way they wanted. This was scrapped in favour of *Angel Station*, possibly in tribute to the central London underground stop of the same name. The original design was also rejected, in favour of artwork showing a design of a staircase around an elevator that owed something to the quasi-surrealist geometrical perspectives of the Swiss artist M.C. Escher. An image of the partly unclothed bat lady on one part of the cover was deemed too explicit, and the hair over her shoulders was accordingly extended so as not to cause offence.

If *Watch* had moved them a little closer towards a pop direction, *Angel Station* subtly continued this trend. Discreet, almost disco basslines and more contemporary keyboard sounds proved that they had kept an ear out for what the newer generation of pop and rock acts were playing. It was arguable that Manfred had helped to invent synth-pop, or rather synth-rock, in the first place. But like other names who had been proud to fly the progressive rock banner at the start of the decade and then gently shifted ground towards pop or even dance, he could keep abreast of present trends without sacrificing that sense of adventure as well as anyone.

Whereas the previous albums had been recorded in the studio at London, this time, they laid down the basic tracks there and then moved west to more relaxed surroundings. The venue was to be Dunowen House, the property of former Jimi Hendrix Experience bass guitarist Noel Redding and his family, near Clonakilty in Ireland. Tom McGuinness knew the area well as he had relations there, and recommended it to Manfred as a good place to work and play. The Reddings were old friends and, in addition to playing host to the group, also allowed them to set up the Manor House Recording Studios, the property of Virgin Records, to bring everything over by articulated truck and set it all up in the grounds. They carried on overdubbing the basic tracks, working in Noel's rehearsal room and feeding out the results through cables to the mobile unit, while maintaining visual contact with each other through a closed-circuit television network.

Neither of the singles reached the Top 40 in Britain, 'You Angel You' stalling at No. 54 and 'Don't Kill it Carol', with the full-length 'Blinded by the Light' on the B-side, No. 45. The latter was aided by another appearance on *Top of the Pops*, and also a limited edition picture disc 7", the uncensored bat lady image passing without any controversy in Britain. Coincidentally, just scraping the Top 40 at the same time was 'One Rule For You' by After The Fire. A former progressive rock quartet noted for their distinctive synthesiser work and now navigating a more commercial musical path, their keyboard player Peter 'Memory' Banks was evidently much influenced by Manfred's playing, with a similar ear for memorable riffs and the facility to bend notes in the same fashion.

Geoff Britton was a gifted musician known for his skills not only on drums but also on alto sax. Unfortunately, he also suffered from recurring glandular fever which prevented him from taking part in the *Angel Station* tour. His place was taken by John Lingwood, previously a member of rock-blues outfit Steamhammer, who had also played on sessions for other artists, including Arthur Brown and Maddy Prior, as well as in musicals in the West End, including *Hair* and *Jesus Christ Superstar*.

The group played no dates in America during 1979, an absence from the concert halls that would be reflected in the record's disappointing stateside success. As they were not there to promote it, it only reached number 144 during a 13-week run. 'You Angel You' did better as a single, with a high of number 58.

On 14 March, they played their first show with Steve Waller and John Lingwood. The occasion was an Easter ball at Keele University as a warm-up for the forthcoming European tour. Eleven dates kept them on the road in Britain throughout most of June, the major one being at Hammersmith Odeon. Journalist Janice Moir singled out 'new boy Steve Waller' for particular praise, noting that 'his powerful voice with its grainy melodic quality' fitted in well with the repertoire. At another date on the tour in Paris, Steve Gett of *Melody Maker* opined that the new guitarist and singer had brought something new to the Band, 'especially on stage where his dynamic lead axe and general good humour have established him as a focal point. When I last saw them, too much emphasis seemed to be placed on vocalist and guitarist Chris Thompson as a frontman, but now the attention has been more evenly distributed.' Yet another (anonymous) reviewer in *Sounds* considered that Steve's more soul-orientated background may not have been the kind of style that would have gelled with the Earth Band's approach any more than his distinctive penguin-like appearance, but he added a swing to the newer songs, although 'he still needs to do some homework on some of the older songs, however, sort out just how and why they have the status they do.'

Some fans felt his bluesy approach and almost growling vocal marked something of a departure for the group that was at odds with their previous style, and on a musical level, he was a less than perfect fit. Yet as a natural showman and extrovert, and with his roguish appearance, he brought a striking sense of personality onstage with him.

The live dates saw a new innovation in their presentation, with the use of cartoons projected onto a large screen behind them. Manfred said he thought it would be entertaining, give the audience's eyes and ears a rest, and felt it would be an interesting change from just acquiring bigger lighting systems and lasers all the time.

Chris had announced his plan to leave afterwards in order to form his own band, Night. It was an amicable decision all round, and Manfred left him a friendly farewell note, reproduced on the sleeve in his own handwriting: 'I wish to thank him for a valuable creative and personal relationship, and wish him every success in the future.' After they had fulfilled their touring commitments in the summer of 1979, the band ceased to exist – but only for a short time.

As for the former members, Chris Slade joined Uriah Heep for one album, then subsequently worked with Gary Numan, David Gilmour and The Firm (alongside Jimmy Page and Paul Rodgers) and Asia. He would however be best remembered for a couple of stints some years apart with AC/DC. Dave Flett joined Thin Lizzy for a while and later became an addictions counsellor in Florida. Colin Pattenden went on to play and tour with various other bands, including Mungo Jerry and their offshoot combo The King Earl Boogie Band, The Jackie Lynton Band, The Nashville Teens, who were still in demand on the live circuit despite a relatively short chart career that stalled in the mid-1960s, and Beggars Opera. He also subsequently founded and managed CP Sound Ltd, an audio system and lighting design and installation company in Surrey.

Manfred Mann's Earth Band was dead – long live Manfred Mann's Earth Band. With a new decade would come new personnel, but the era of a reasonably static line-up would be a thing of the past, in favour of a more revolving door principle. Like many other bands of their generation, they would take occasional sabbaticals until the faithful began to wonder if they had split or were merely resting. But over the years, they would take time out for separate projects with other artists yet still raise the collective flag time and time again, in the process becoming an almost permanent fixture of Britain's rock heritage.

Right and below: Manfred Mann and Steve Waller promoting 'Don't Kill it Carol', their final top 50 UK hit, on *Top of the Pops* in July 1979.

Right: The group on stage during their extensive UK and European tours from March to June 1979.

Left: Drummer Geoff Britton, who played on *Angel Station* but was unable to tour with the group for health reasons.

MANFRED MANN'S EARTH BAND

Above: The group in 1979, shortly before their relatively stable line-up gave way to a revolving door principle from 1980 onwards.

Postscript: 1980-2020 - Beyond Earth and back again

The 1970s had undoubtedly been Manfred Mann's Earth Band's best decade. During the early 1980s onwards, they had three Top 10 albums in Norway, two in Germany (always their favourite market) and a third in the Top 20, while in America, two reached the Top 100. In Britain, only one album would manage a solitary week in the lower reaches of the Top 100. Nevertheless, they still released new material at a steady rate, and maintained a regular schedule of live appearances.

Chris Thompson's imminent departure spurred Manfred into looking for a new vocalist to replace him and began holding auditions. Among the hopefuls were Graham Bonnet, formerly of The Marbles and more recently Rainbow, Pete French from Atomic Rooster, and Brian Johnson from Geordie. Not long afterwards, Brian later auditioned for and was accepted by AC/DC when they needed a new vocalist after the sudden death of Bon Scott.

Another one considered for the Earth Band vacancy was the sole American contender on the list, Huey Lewis. He had played harmonica with Chris Thompson in Filthy McNasty and also been a member of contemporary pub rock outfit The Dire Ear Band, a part-time venture made up largely of members of Thin Lizzy with Nick Lowe that later recruited The Sex Pistols' Steve Jones and Paul Cook, becoming The Greedy Bastards (subsequently The Greedies). Huey had also contributed to albums by Thin Lizzy, Dave Edmunds and Nick Lowe. According to various sources, he was at first a prime contender, until he declined the offer and went off to form his own outfit, Huey Lewis and The News. Manfred later commented that he rejected Huey because he wasn't especially good on that particular day. An advert was placed in *Melody Maker* inviting demo tapes, which promptly came in their hundreds. Faced with the nightmare scenario that sifting through such a collection would have entailed, Manfred contacted Chris Thompson to reconsider his position once more.

Chris achieved modest success with Night in America, but less in Britain, and the band thus became a part-time commitment throughout their brief existence. They released an album in 1979 and another the next, but with less success than anticipated. As a result, he found it would be feasible to combine his career with them while continuing with Manfred Mann's Earth Band at the same time, and the auditions for those others proved unnecessary. Even so, it was to become apparent that *Angel Station* and the tour to promote it had marked a decisive chapter in the history of Manfred Mann's Earth Band. They gradually became what some saw as an equivalent of The Alan Parsons Project, with Manfred at the helm directing a group comprising largely session singers and players.

The first album issued under their name during the 1980s, *Chance*, was the result of sessions between May 1979 and July 1980. Supplementing Chris Thompson, Steve Waller and Manfred himself on vocals were Peter Marsh, formerly of Easy Street, Willy Finlayson from Bees Make Honey and Meal Ticket, and Dyan Birch. In addition to Steve, four other guitarists were featured. Mick Rogers returned to help out, while Trevor Rabin, a South African musician who subsequently worked with Yes, Geoff Whitehorn, formerly of Back Street Crawler, and Robbie McIntosh, part of Night with Chris Thompson, were also featured. Two singles were released, 'Lies (Through the 80s')' and their version of another Bruce Springsteen song, 'For You' were released but had more success in America, as did the album.

In January 1981, they returned to live work. During the first three months of 1981, they undertook the 'Chance' tour, starting with two dates in England in January and concluding with the final two in England at the end of March, the rest at various venues on mainland Europe.

Pat King left the group after the tour but retained his connections with them, and for over 20 years, he worked as their lighting designer. Later he moved to Spain and died after a heart attack in January 2022. He was replaced in what was becoming a fairly fluid line-up by Matt Irving, a former member of The Babys.

A stand-alone single appeared in November 1981, an electro-disco version of 'I (Who Have Nothing)'. It had originally been an American hit for Ben E. King, and subsequently a British Top 10 smash for Shirley Bassey, a lesser success in subsequent years on separate occasions for Tom Jones and Sylvester, and also the debut single for The Spectres, a mid-1960s line-up of the group that would later become Status Quo. Featuring the vocals of Steve Waller and Shona Laing, a New Zealand singer who was to become a member of the group for a couple of years, the Earth Band's retread, which reflected an awareness of 1980s electro-disco styles, became a top 50 hit in Germany but made no waves anywhere else. Although at first glance it might have seemed a strange choice of song for them, Manfred enjoyed the challenge of tackling the unexpected. He said he liked their version 'because it was such a strange way of doing the song'. Initially, they arranged for Steve and Shona to sing separately, then realised that to put them together singing different parts of the song instead made the result much better. John Lingwood initially thought it a bad idea to cover the song, but time proved him wrong, and he thought the combination of both vocalists worked really well. Not everyone agreed, and he always remembered one review of the time in the music papers that said their version had as much charm as a multiple pile-up on a motorway.

Perhaps because it was such a departure from their usual style, it was and always remained one of Steve's favourite recordings from his days with them. Had it received enough airplay in Britain or America, it could have been one of those off-the-wall hits that would have surprised many of their fans, perhaps for the better, perhaps for the worse.

The next album, *Somewhere in Afrika*, was released in Germany in October 1982 (hence the different spelling of 'Africa' as the group had always been so popular in Germany, Afrika being the German spelling) and in Britain early the following year. Using South African field recordings, a forerunner of similar experiments that would appear on later records by Paul Simon and Peter Gabriel, it included the group's versions of Sting's 'Demolition Man', Bob Marley's 'Redemption Song', and Al Stewart's 'Eyes of Nostradamus'.

Whereas most established groups would routinely issue live albums from time to time, often featuring several of their greatest hits, during the 1970s, Manfred Mann's Earth Band had taken an almost reverse path. Several of their albums had been more or less studio recordings, including the occasional live track or jam, sometimes overdubbed and altered in the studio. In 1982 he told Greg Russo that they had often been persuaded to release a live album as they always went down so well onstage. For a long time, he resisted doing so, as he insisted that they were in their element live when an audience was there watching as well as listening to them, savouring the full experience of seeing them and enjoying the full visuals of the lights and other special effects. He felt that the tapes were simply not good enough when they played them back afterwards and that whenever he listened to a record, the dynamics were destroyed. Their enormous changes of volume, from very quiet to very loud and back again, didn't come across effectively.

Yet after more than a decade, he bowed to demand. The 1983 'Somewhere in Europe' tour, promoting the album *Somewhere in Afrika*, was released on an in-concert album the following year, *Budapest Live*. The title was slightly misleading as only a minority of the recordings came from a couple of dates at Budapest Sporthalle in April 1982, and the rest from a show at the Dominion Theatre, London, a week later. It contained no surprises, just a selection of eight of their greatest hits and best-known singles, including 'Spirits in the Night', 'Demolition Man', 'Davy's on the Road Again', 'Blinded by the Light', and 'Lies (Through the 80s)'.

During the next three years, the regular personnel changes continued, with Steve Waller and Matt Irving leaving after two shows at the Dominion Theatre in April 1983. Steve had become well known and respected for his good humour, personality and friendly banter onstage, to say nothing of a somewhat Roy Wood meets Rasputin-like appearance with his full beard. He was also a liability for the group because of his heavy drinking, and Manfred asked him to leave. Returning to the South London pub circuit, he never became a member of a major act again but was content to carry on working around the London pub gig circuit with Steve Waller's Overload, becoming known affectionately as the 'Lowell George of South London'. To the end, he retained fond memories of his stint in the Earth Band. He died in February 2000 from liver problems, aged 48, the first former member of the band to pass away.

Matt undertook session work with Roger Waters and Squeeze, and formed Los Pacaminos with Paul Young (of 'Wherever I Lay My Hat' fame). He died in April 2015 from prostate cancer aged 65. Six months later, Jack Bruce, who had briefly been a member of the old band, died at the age of 71.

The band took a break from live work for nearly three years. During this period, they recorded and released 'Runner', written by Canadian singer-songwriter Ian Thomas, in memory of Terry Fox, a cancer victim who had started to run across Canada to bring attention to and raise funds for cancer awareness but died before he was able to complete the journey. Released in America in January 1984, it reached No. 22, their most successful record there since 'Blinded by the Light' – and what would be their last chart single. It was also featured in the science fiction movie *The Philadelphia Experiment* later that year. Appearing in Britain in March, it failed completely.

By this time, their together activities were slowing down. In March 1986, Steve Kinch joined on bass. Bronze Records had recently gone into liquidation after experiencing financial problems, and they signed with 10 Records. The next album, *Criminal Tango*, later that year, included

Chris Thompson and the returning Mick Rogers together, although the former was on vocals and the latter guitars, but sang very little.

Mick put down his departure to what was probably a midlife musician crisis. After leaving ten years earlier, he had returned to Australia to get together with some friends who were fusion players, thus allowing him the best of both worlds. One moment, he said, they would be doing Ornette Coleman, and the next he was doing something from the 1950s, usually old Elvis. Over the next few years, he formed a new group Aviator with ex-Jethro Tull drummer Clive Bunker and former Blodwyn Pig saxophonist Mick Abrahams, who released two albums before disbanding. He spent a while in Los Angeles, 'got the muso stuff out of [his] system', rejoined the Earth Band in 1986 and has remained a member to this day.

Criminal Tango was a deliberate attempt to sound more relevant to the American market, but ironically US Virgin rejected it. Some music industry insiders saw them as dinosaurs, leftovers from the progressive rock age who had failed to remain relevant to the image-conscious 1980s. On its British release, the reviews were poor, with most critics finding the kindest thing to say about it was that it sounded like a typical 1980s keyboard-orientated AOR set, and it sold poorly. So did the single, a new take on The Rods' 1977 Top 10 hit 'Do Anything You Wanna Do' with prominent keyboards and children's chorus that seemed a strange choice, lacking the sheer urgency of and comparing badly with the high-spirited, in-your-face original. Other covers were featured, the best of them being an atmospheric version of Joni Mitchell's 'Banquet'. Enjoyable enough, although nothing special, was a cover of The Beatles' 'Hey Bulldog', renamed 'Bulldog', saved mainly by Mick's ace guitar work. At last, the group had tackled a Fab Four song, and to their credit, they were enterprising enough to choose one of the most obscure of them all. They also included a rendition of The Jam's 'Going Underground', although theirs was much slower than the original and rearranged into something resembling a power ballad with shades of Bruce Springsteen. In the more image-conscious sections of the British music press, for a prog rock band with their roots in the 1960s and early 1970s to record hits by The Jam and The Rods was unlikely to be seen as a credible move.

Their tour that year saw them include a song that they never committed to record, or at least as a studio recording, The Spencer Davis Group's 'Gimme Some Lovin''. They made their final British appearance at the Old School House, Woking, on 19 August. A few further dates in

Germany were completed with a show in Munich on 7 September. It would be over four years before they took to the stage again.

For the next album, *Masque*, the group were reduced to a trio of Manfred, Mick Rogers and John Lingwood. They were supplemented by several outside musicians, including Maggie Ryder and Linda Taylor on vocals, Mark Feltham of Nine Below Zero on harmonica, plus three bassists, several trumpet and saxophone players, and Anthony Moore on programming. Unusually for the group, despite a total playing time of just under 40 minutes, this album contained 12 tracks – several remarkably short by their usual standards, and with some sounding unusually undeveloped. It was also a strange collection of styles. Some of it borrowed from 1940s-style pop and big band swing, using elements of tunes from Charlie Parker and Horace Silver, while some presented rock-classics fusion with further adaptations of Gustav Holst's music, including a new, almost electro-pop and rather lightweight (not to say rather unnecessary) retread of 'Joybringer' and well as 'Hymn (from Jupiter)', the tune more widely known as 'I Vow to Thee My Country'. Since the days of *Solar Fire* and 'Joybringer', the copyright on Holst's compositions had expired, and now they had entered the public domain, Manfred was free to take from them at his leisure.

For once, the cover versions did not venture towards the Dylan or Springsteen songbooks, but they offered their own take on 'What You Give Is What You Get', otherwise known as The Jam's 'Start', Cream's 'We're Going Wrong' on which Mick sounded remarkably like Jack Bruce on the original, and Michael Martin Murphey's 'Geronimo's Cadillac', a song about how the Native Americans had been deceived over the years by false promises and broken treaties. It had been performed by many others since the writer's own recording in 1972, the best known being one by Cher about three years later.

The album sold badly again, and even in Germany, where the group had retained a faithful fan base, reception was particularly disappointing. It was a frustrating time for Manfred, especially as his efforts to form a band with Greg Lake on vocals, plus a guitarist and drummer came to nothing. Soon afterwards, there was a major fire at the Workhouse, his studio, with a catastrophic loss of equipment and recordings. As time would tell, some of his archival material had fortunately been stored elsewhere and later came to light.

For four years, Manfred Mann's Earth Band was not exactly disbanded but in limbo. Feeling sorely in need of a new direction,

Manfred acquired a songbook of American Indian tribal chants. As he had recently been doing what he regarded as 'straight commercial pop music' and suddenly felt he did not want to be doing it any longer, he began to experiment with music from the book. Although he knew nothing about North American culture, the melodies fascinated him. Soon after that, he was going to visit his family in South Africa and he took with him a tape made by a musician who played African hunting bows and other similar instruments. From listening to this, while he was in Johannesburg, the idea gradually took shape, and he began recording a very different kind of music.

To assist him, he called on a group of players based mainly in South Africa, plus saxophone player Barbara Thompson, with whom he had already worked while he was in England. Additional musicians and backing vocals were invited to contribute, and the result was a collection of music based on the melodies of four Native American tribes and one African tribe. Most of it was recorded live in the studio in South Africa, with only one track being produced in England, using samplers and associated technology.

Manfred Mann's *Plains Music* was released in Europe, South Africa and America in 1991 and in Britain the following year. He stressed that it was not meant to be in any sense representative of the original ethnic music that had been its source material. His aim was to make a simple album of plain music, using as few notes as possible and keeping the tracks short and to the point. Most of them were credited as 'traditional, arranged by Manfred Mann', with one including lyrics by Mike Heron.

Having satisfied his creative instincts with the album, he returned to his roots by reforming the Earth Band with Mick Rogers, Steve Kinch on bass, vocalist Noel McCalla and drummer Clive Bunker, who had worked with Mick in Aviator. Also returning was Chris Thompson, who had been busy with several solo ventures in the intervening years, as well as being one of four co-writers of 'You're the Voice', a worldwide hit for John Farnham in 1987. Another of the song's joint writers was Maggie Ryder, who had worked alongside Chris in helping to supply backing vocals for Queen at the Freddie Mercury Tribute Concert in 1992, with both subsequently reprising the same role while on tour with The Brian May Band later that year. Nearly every year from 1991 onwards, they toured Europe, with a few British dates as well, always playing to packed venues. Audiences could be guaranteed a first-rate show every time with a selection of old tried and trusted favourites, new numbers and the occasional cover version. Although they were used to seeing Manfred dancing happily in front of his keyboards, on occasion, they would be delighted during part of the 'Gimme Some Lovin'/'Mony Mony' segue when he left his instrument and moved around the stage with the vigour of a man half his age.

By this time, albums from nearly all established acts were few and far between, unlike the more frenetic pace at which one new release had followed another around 20 years earlier. In 1992 Manfred observed with some irony that in the early 1960s, they used to make records in three hours. Three decades on, everything had improved to such an extent, with far more facilities than they had ever dreamed possible in the early days, 'and it's all so much faster with technology that it only takes two months'. Now that they had control over every parameter, he said that 'the worst thing that's happened is that you've got too much control.' He was not alone among recording artists in realising that having more facilities at his disposal did not automatically mean that everything could be done more quickly. On the contrary, the ability to do anything within reason in the studio and that never-ending striving for absolute perfection had merely slowed the whole process down to a degree that.

The next album was recorded over four years at the restored Workhouse Studios, and must have been the one that they had been waiting to make for a long time. Unusually for them, *Soft Vengeance*, released in June 1996, was a long album, and instead of falling well short of 40 minutes of playing time, it contained around 55 minutes, with a total of 14 tracks. On some of the mid-1970s albums, it was arguable that as his own producer, Manfred gave some of the tracks a little too long to breathe and they outstayed their welcome. Twenty years later, the opposite was true in that some of them seemed far too short, and simply did not have time to get into top gear or develop properly before they were cut or faded.

Original material was, as usual, at a premium, with only three numbers written or co-written by Manfred, two being very short and the third, 'Adults Only', an unexceptional instrumental. The most notable cover versions were 'Pleasure and Pain', a song by Mike Chapman and Holly Knight that had been a hit for Divinyls in America and their native Australia, though never released in Britain, a dramatic retread of Del Amitri's world-weary contemporary classic 'Nothing Ever Happens' and a very relaxed 'Shelter From the Storm' (interpolating a brief snatch of

'Joybringer'), from Dylan's *Blood on the Tracks*. Less impressive was
a raid on the early Rolling Stones' B-sides catalogue, a synth-pop cod-
reggae stab at 'Play With Fire' that sounded rather bland beside the
original. Overall, the album contained some interesting songs, but heavy
reliance on electronic drums and wash of synthesisers throughout, as
opposed to Manfred's more spirited Moog work that was one of their
calling cards in the early days, let it down in its desperation to sound
contemporary and ultra-1990s. It reached No. 65 on the German charts
but never managed to register anywhere else.

Clive Bunker left shortly after its release and was replaced on drums
by John Trotter. The six-piece band toured Europe, and recordings made
while they were on the road resulted in a double live album in 1998,
Mann Alive. The first disc was titled 'The Gig' and the second 'Encore &
More'. Five Dylan songs were included, 'You Angel You', 'Father of Day,
Father of Night', 'Shelter From the Storm', inevitably 'Mighty Quinn', and
also 'The Times They Are A-Changin''. There was nothing from the pre-
1976 Earth Band albums, with 'Blinded by the Light', another of those
songs they simply could not omit, being the earliest featured.

The last album to date in a group career that had begun in 1971 came
six years later. *Manfred Mann '06* was released in 2004 under a title
that was deliberately an anachronism because he said he found the
concept 'artistically interesting'. Although billed as 'Manfred Mann with
Manfred Mann's Earth Band', he regarded it as really a solo project.
In the sleeve notes, he explained that some numbers were recorded
in a more unrehearsed and experimental way than the others, and he,
therefore, wanted to release it outside the normal Earth Band context,
as representative only of his personal tastes and not those of his fellow
group members.

It is certainly a strange business, sounding more like a scattershot
collection of experiments and not fully realised ideas. Some online
reviewers likened it to an album of demos, sorely in need of an outside
producer. Manfred seemed to be lurching in several directions, from
electro-pop to sampling to rap, then going in search of the classics,
and then back again. To call it a chaotic mess would be uncharitable,
but the old phrase about the chameleon exploding when he stepped
onto a tartan rug springs to mind. Of the 14 tracks, only three exceed
the four-minute mark, with several considerably less. It is as if he is
tinkering with one idea, taking it only so far, and then dashing on to
the next. The opening and closing tracks, 'Demons and Dragons' and

'Dragons (Reprise)', are based on a Super Furry Animals song, with lyrics by Paddy McAloon of Prefab Sprout, and feature crooning vocals from Thomas D, rapper with German hip hop outfit Die Fantastischen Vier. His love of the classics surfaced in 'Mars', a return to the music of Gustav Holst, although this time it was severely mangled in electronic trickery that sounds as if Gary Numan or Kraftwerk may have been involved or sampled somewhere. Tchaikovsky was given a joint composing credit for the song 'Independent Woman' and the instrumental fragment 'Marche Slave'. There are two more or less spoken numbers, the old Coasters' Leiber-Stoller penned 1950s hit, 'Down in Mexico', and 'Frog', a Hans Christian Andersen-style story recited with an acoustic guitar and an ersatz heavenly wordless warbling in the background. Elsewhere there were various songs on which ethereal synths and programmed drumming take over – all very contemporary but horribly soulless. One instrumental, 'Happenstance', had an oriental flavour that could have been developed into something more interesting, while another, 'Black Eyes', a slow moody piece in Pink Floyd mode, did at least boast Mick Rogers on guitar, and also sounded like the drums were played by a human (in this case Geoff Dunn) and not by a computer, as seemed the case on several of the others.

Overall, the most charitable thing that can be said about this album is that Manfred was not afraid to take chances. It's his album or his party, and he can try the patience of his 1970s fans if he wants to. But for many of those fans, it may not stand up to repeated listening.

Around this time, a couple of Earth Band tracks received a new lease of life in the modern world with two separate dance remixes of their versions of Bruce Springsteen songs. The first was a remix of 'For You', credited to The Disco Boys featuring Manfred Mann's Earth Band. The Disco Boys were a German house music DJ and production duo from Hamburg: Raphael Krickow and Gordon Hollenga. It was initially released in 2005 and was an immediate hit in Germany, but proved more successful when reactivated two years later. This coincided with an even higher-charting remix of 'Blinded by the Light', credited to Michael Mind featuring Manfred Mann's Earth Band. The Michael Mind Project was the brainchild of Jens Kindervater, and Francois Sanders, an electro-house partnership based in Aachen, Germany. It topped the German dance charts for several weeks and made the German top 20.

After a four-year stint with the band, John Trotter left in 2000 to be replaced by Richard Marcangelo. Two years later, he was replaced by Pete

May and then Geoff Dunn until 2007. Jimmy Copley took over until 2015, when he was diagnosed with leukaemia (and died in 2017), resulting in the return of John Lingwood. Chris Thompson came back to the band in 1996 alongside Mick Rogers and Noel McCalla until 1999, then again for a short period in 2004. Like Mick, he had had a remarkable see-saw history of band membership. In his words, he 'kind of left in inverted commas, because I left them, then I went back, left them, and went back right up until 1999. Manfred took so long to make albums that I would have gone crazy doing nothing.' Noel was replaced as vocalist in 2009 by Peter Cox, formerly of Go West (and, before that, in the short-lived Terra Nova with Chris Slade and Colin Pattenden), and he left in 2011 to be followed by Robert Hart, formerly vocalist with Bad Company.

Compilations of the 'ultimate collection' variety continued to appear at intervals. The most successful was a TV-advertised 18-track CD with minimalist packaging, clearly aimed more at the casual consumer in the petrol station forecourt shop than at the more discerning collector, *The Very Best Of MMEB*, released by Arcade in 1994. It spent one week in the British charts at No. 69. With the exception of 'Joybringer', the track it could not omit, it focused largely on the Top 75 entries from the second half of the decade and a handful of more recent tracks, up to and including the non-album single 'The Runner'.

By the 21st century, several acts of a similar vintage had accumulated enough alternative versions and rarities in the vaults to warrant a comprehensive and suitably well-researched multi-disc anthology sooner or later, and in August 2005, it was the turn of the Earth Band. *Odds & Sods: Mis-takes & Out-takes* consists of four CDs, much of it buried treasure from the vaults. The first three comprise previously unissued versions of tracks from two 'lost' LPs. One was the unreleased Manfred Mann Chapter Three third and final album, including the original version of 'Messin' Up the Land' with Mike Hugg on vocals. It had been presumed destroyed in the Workhouse Studios fire until another copy was located among tapes in the American record company offices. The other was *Stepping Sideways,* the debut Earth Band album that was scrapped and partially re-recorded. The fourth includes unreleased studio material, including new versions of The Lovin' Spoonful's 'Summer in the City' from 1987, planned as a tentative single and then shelved, and of ABBA's 'SOS', recorded in 2001 with Noel McCalla on vocals, and live performances. In December 2006 came the DVD *Unearthed 1973–2005: The Best of Manfred Mann's Earth Band,* with 20 tracks ranging from three recorded in Sweden in 1973 ('Father of Day', 'Captain Bobby Stout' and 'Black & Blue') to a 2005 'Mighty Quinn'.

Five years later, to celebrate the group's 40th anniversary, arrived a box set of 18 Manfred Mann's Earth Band CDs, plus two previously unreleased bonus discs. One was an in-concert set recorded in Germany in July 2011, *Live in Ersingen 2011*. The first album to feature Robert Hart on vocals, it included another Bruce Springsteen cover, 'Dancing in the Dark', which teased the audience by interpolating lines from 'The House of the Rising Sun' at the beginning, and an 11-minute 'Mighty Quinn', which featured a few bars of the 'Smoke on the Water' riff from Manfred on the keys. The other was *Leftovers,* a selection of 7" versions, alternate edits and mixes. Also included in the package was a booklet, a double-sided poster, and an 'exclusive casebound collection of Manfred's short stories'.

At intervals, generous helpings of live recordings were made available. *The Bootleg Archive*, Vols. 1–5, released in 2009, consisted of material recorded on various European tours between 1981 and 2007. It was joined eight years later by Vols. 6–10, another quintuple package, made up of more of the same covering the years between 1991 and 2014. Most tracks were already familiar to those who owned the previous records, but there were a few making it on to record with the artists' full approval for the first time, with the second set including a stripped-down version of 'Do Wah Diddy Diddy' featuring punters enthusiastically singing along (how long can you disown a pop song that might have a dumb title but still makes people smile?), and T. Rex's 'Get It On'.

Two years later, the BBC archives were raided for *Radio Days*, covering the entire Manfred Mann career. The first disc covered the Paul Jones era, and the second that of Michael d'Abo. Number three, 'Radio Days and Rarities' embraced the shorter Chapter Three era, supplemented with the film soundtrack work undertaken by Manfred and Mike Hugg in the last few months of the old group. All were single CDs, the music supplemented by Brian Matthew's interviews with the full group and individual members. To complete the series was a double CD covering the Earth Band, including the early sessions and a recording originally broadcast as part of the Radio 1 In Concert series. On the back of the CD, Manfred, who had long been known as an exacting interviewee who did not always suffer fools gladly, paid a generous tribute to Brian, who had presented Radio 2's long-established

Sounds of the Sixties until just before his death in 2017 at the age of 88. Brian, said Manfred, was the most educated and informed interviewer he had ever met. His research was always thorough and meticulous, and his achievements and role were perhaps never sufficiently recognised as he didn't cultivate a 'cheeky chappie' persona beloved by several of his fellow radio DJs.

To celebrate the group's 50th anniversary in 2021 came *Mannthology*, a deluxe package consisting of an LP-size hardback book containing four CDs and two DVDs. The first three included singles released in Britain, Europe and America, some on CD for the first time, while the fourth was given over to 12" and alternative versions, all specially remastered. A few recent recordings, including versions of Springsteen's 'Lost in the Flood' (yet another song from his debut album) and Leonard Cohen's 'Bird on the Wire', were to be included but then held over for a possible future release. The first DVD was a nine-track in-concert recording made in Switzerland in October 2017, *Live at Baloise Session*, basically a greatest hits offering, while the final one was a documentary about the group, including archive footage and specially recorded interviews. The accompanying 100-page book included a history of the group with recollections and photographs. Such was the longevity and loyalty of the band's fan base in Germany that public demand resulted in the appearance of a vinyl edition alongside the CDs, and despite a hefty price tag it still entered the charts there at No. 21, although only staying for one week.

All these records were released through Creature Music, set up by Manfred and the management in association with Steve Fernie of East Central One to acquire the group's back catalogue and maintain full control over reissues. In 2017 the company also purchased the rights to the 1960s recordings, as well as the Earth Band albums previously owned by Warner Bros in America.

Manfred Mann's Earth Band has remained in existence over the years, with fluctuating personnel and the occasional hiatus – like The Rolling Stones, Fleetwood Mac, Deep Purple and a few others. As he told his biographer Greg Russo in the mid-1990s, it was no longer a small compact unit of four musicians and had not been so for a very long time. 'It's not a band as such, it's a name for a group of people that are working together.' Professional musicians rarely retire, and unless they decide on a complete career change generally continue to pursue their vocation until old age and ill health. He intended to continue as long as he felt like doing so, and as long as it was feasible. 'It's not a problem to go to a studio and make music. The problem is people may not buy or like it. If it makes it, you might as well do it. There's no reason to stop now.' Twenty years or more later, the new records were still coming, but more slowly. By the 1990s, he was no longer focused on trying to have hit records, only hit albums as far as possible, and he had the good fortune of having a loyal fan base in Europe, where sales remained buoyant for a long time.

It was inevitable that over the course of time, the rate of release of new albums would slow down to a trickle. While music streaming affected recording artists as the coronavirus pandemic brought live work to a halt in February 2020 for a couple of years, its practitioners continued to create and record in isolation with all the benefits of modern technology in their home studios as best they could. Moreover, recording complete albums was hard work. By the time he had reached his seventies, Manfred said he did not plan to make albums anymore, just individual tracks – 'I will start releasing one track at a time, I think.'

Yet live work had always been and remained their strongest calling card. They did better concerts than records, he said, and they were much more powerful and dynamic on the stage. It was one aspect of his work that had never changed during five decades in the music business, and he continued to maintain that in a band situation, he felt they sounded better live than in the studio. He was content with what he was doing, although when asked about the rise of Spotify and music streaming, he admitted it had a serious downside, not for people like him but for newer artists who were struggling to establish themselves. For him, it was a great shame that consumers, particularly those who had been born and raised in the 21st century in a world where an internet connection was taken for granted, were getting used to the idea that they no longer had to buy music. It all impacted severely on creative artists and performers, who would 'end up doing a job where nobody thinks you should pay for the job you're doing'.

Chris Thompson agreed that it was increasingly difficult in the modern age for young people to get a band together and be successful. In the 1960s and 1970s, radio would always play a wide variety of music, particularly in America. While they could always take advantage of modern facilities at home, nowadays, it was far harder for them to get exposure and reach a wider audience. They might have a chance to make one or two singles, but 'if it doesn't work, then – out the door. And that's no good for artists' development, no good for songwriting development, it's no good for band development.'

As for the former members of Manfred Mann in the 1960s, they all pursued active careers in the music business, some maintaining strong links with their work in the 1960s. Mike Hugg had returned to the top 40 in 1973 with 'Whatever Happened to You', credited to Highly Likely and the theme song from the BBC situation comedy *Whatever Happened to the Likely Lads?* which he co-wrote with Ian La Frenais, one of the scriptwriters, and co-produced with Dave Hadfield. Veteran session singer Tony Rivers, formerly of one-hit wonders Harmony Grass, was the uncredited vocalist. Tom McGuinness co-founded McGuinness Flint with former John Mayall's Bluesbreakers drummer Hughie Flint, who had provided occasional percussion for Manfred Mann in the late 1960s, with songwriting duo Benny Gallagher and Graham Lyle, and singer Dennis Coulson. After two trailblazing folk-rock singles, 'When I'm Dead and Gone' and 'Malt and Barley Blues', which made the top five, and a top ten debut album, they lost momentum with various personnel changes. *Lo and Behold*, co-produced by Manfred Mann, was critically well-received, but subsequent singles and albums failed, and they disbanded in 1974. Tom McGuinness and the group's keyboard player Lou Stonebridge formed a new band Stonebridge McGuinness, which recorded four singles later in the decade, had a minor hit in 1979 with 'Oo-Eeh Baby' which led to an appearance on *Top of the Pops*, and an album *Corporate Madness*.

Paul Jones had the most varied career of all. After a series of pop singles in the late 1960s, including two top 10 hits at the beginning with 'High Time' and 'I've Been a Bad, Bad Boy', he also branched out into acting on stage and screen. His solo records and albums were nothing if not eclectic. After a few run-of-the-mill pop albums in the late 1960s, he went to America for a few years and completely changed direction. His 1971 album *Crucifix in a Horseshoe* – significantly released on the Vertigo label, briefly home to the Earth Band as well – veered between progressive country rock, jazz and folk, and although neglected at the time, it is now regarded as something of a classic. He also appeared in musicals on stage and album, including *Evita* and *Joseph and the Amazing Technicolor Dreamcoat*, and made solo singles on various labels that encompassed commercial pop, out-and-out disco, and one featuring heavily orchestrated ballad versions of 'Pretty Vacant' and

'Sheena is a Punk Rocker' on either side. Later, he also became a regular radio presenter, the high spot of which was a weekly blues show on Radio 2 that he took over from Alexis Korner after the latter retired due to ill health, and presented for over 30 years. An even more durable achievement was his foundation and fronting of The Blues Band, which also included Tom McGuinness, Hughie Flint (later replaced by ex-Family drummer Rob Townsend), guitarist Dave Kelly and bass guitarist Gary Fletcher. Formed in 1979, they charted with their first three albums and also an EP. They disbanded in 1983 but later re-formed and, to quote a subsequent album title of theirs, were *Back for More*.

So, almost, were the old Manfred Mann. A reunion of the old group was planned for April 1983 to be recorded and filmed at the Marquee in London, but Manfred himself did not want to be involved and the plan was cancelled. Manfred said he had no issue with other 1960s bands like The Searchers or The Tremeloes re-forming or supplementing themselves with newer members to play their greatest hits night after night, but it was not for him. 'I just feel that you can't actually recreate what's gone before – the moment is gone and it had its strengths and weaknesses.' He preferred to carry on making new music, changing all the time. Trying to reproduce what he had done nearly 20 years earlier, he said, would be embarrassing, and 'mainly a nostalgia trip'.

Nevertheless, the rest of them got together to celebrate Tom McGuinness's 50th birthday one evening in December 1991, at the Town & Country Club, London. Manfred Mann's Earth Band were touring Germany at the time, but The Blues Band, Gallagher & Lyle, Tom Robinson and Noel Redding were there. The impromptu performance they put on was such a success that they decided some of them would continue playing live on a regular basis as long as audiences were still interested in coming to see them. From then on, The Manfreds – deliberately named thus out of deference to their former keyboard player, who firmly declined to participate – became a regular fixture on the live music circuit, with Paul Jones, Tom McGuinness and Rob Townsend as members of the group, plus Mike Hugg, (sometimes) Michael d'Abo, with Benny Gallagher, later replaced by Marcus Cliffe on bass, and Simon Currie on saxophone and flute. In the meantime, Paul, Tom and Rob continued to record and tour with guitarist/vocalist Dave Kelly and bassist Gary Fletcher as The Blues Band. By early 2022, The Manfreds and The Blues Band were announcing dates for what were intended to be their farewell tours.

Meanwhile, Manfred Mann's Earth Band continued to play live throughout the first two decades of the 21st century, with a few appearances in Britain but the majority in Germany and throughout the rest of Europe. The last pre-pandemic gigs were at major German venues up to mid-February 2020, featuring a set list of tried and trusted favourites, generally opening with 'Captain Bobby Stout', followed by 'Don't Kill it Carol', 'Martha's Madman', 'Demolition Man', 'For You', 'Blinded by the Light', Davy's On the Road Again', 'Father of Day, Father of Night', a cover of Melissa Etheridge's 'Stronger Than Me', and encores of 'Do Wah Diddy Diddy' and 'Mighty Quinn'. The latter song featured in almost every concert they played since forming in 1971, and by 2020 they estimated that during the (almost) half-century that had elapsed since then, it had been performed by them just under 1,900 times.

Although Manfred had sometimes spoken scathingly of the old group's 1960s hits, his views mellowed over time, and he said that now he wasn't averse in principle to playing some of them. They had experimented with one or two of the others but dropped them for various reasons. 'If You Gotta Go, Go Now' was one example; 'even though it's not really a pretty pop song, it just came over with no energy'.

Early in 2020, the coronavirus pandemic struck, with remaining dates having to be rescheduled and then cancelled altogether, alongside a promise of returning once normal service could be resumed. When global restrictions were cautiously lifted at the beginning of 2022, the Earth Band's website announced that Manfred, who had moved to Sweden in 2019 and celebrated his 80th birthday the following year, planned to appear with the group in Europe, while the Earth Band with a new keyboard and synth player were scheduled to play at a forthcoming festival in Great Yarmouth in 2023. On the agenda were also dates in Germany in December 2022 as special guests of Status Quo, all postponed from two years earlier. At his time of life, it was assumed that Manfred would soon retire from live performance. Simultaneously there was tentative talk of a new album, the result of his work on new tracks during the lockdown.

By then, Mick Rogers had become the longest-serving member apart from Manfred himself while devoting himself to other musical activities during the times in between. Among them were sessions for Andy Bown of Status Quo, on his solo album *Unfinished Business*. 'Mick is a typical musician who would play something,' said Andy with a laugh, 'then I'd say, play it again, and he would go, play what? That's where pro tools came in!' Mick also released two solo albums himself, *Back to Earth* in 2002 and *Sharabang* 11 years later. After that, he and Colin Pattenden put together a new outfit, Solar Fire, to play material from the early Earth Band repertoire. The line-up was also to include American musicians Steve Vai and Mike Keneally, both of whom had played with Frank Zappa, on guitar and keyboards, and German jazz drummer Dieter Schroeder. Plans were put on hold initially by the pandemic, and then by Mick's rejoining the original group for live dates in Europe after restrictions were lifted. As this book was going to press, Colin confirmed to the present author that the project still hung in the balance, but 'we can always hope'.

Chris Slade had joined AC/DC in 1989 for four years before being replaced by returning original member Phil Rudd, then played with Asia for seven years. Another stint with AC/DC from 2015 to 2020 followed. He subsequently formed his own outfit, The Chris Slade Timeline, featuring guest musicians and playing music from the various bands in which he had been involved during his career spanning more than half a century. Chris Thompson remained similarly active, writing songs with and for others, fronting his own band, working on a musical with his wife, and also planning what would be a final series of concerts after the pandemic.

By then, the musician and bandleader who had brought everyone together and who described himself modestly in 1979 as 'a bit of a craftsman with a lack of flair but keeps working away and seems to do well', had been plying his craft for around 60 years. In the process, he had become what looked like becoming a more or less indefinite figure on the music scene from the pre-British beat boom era of the early 1960s to long past the millennium well into the fragmented 2020s, and still with more to offer. Speaking in an interview for a history of the group released on DVD, he said that the only aim anyone could have in the music business was to survive; it was like a thousand people trying to get into a lifeboat when the ship is sinking. 'I have no ambition just beyond continuing to play music successfully and earning a living at it.'

Resources

Books
Bainton, R., *Talk To Me Baby: The Story of The Blues Band* (Poole: Firebird, 1994)

Garner, K., *The Peel Sessions* (London: BBC, 2007)

McGuinness, T., *So You Want To Be a Rock 'n' Roll Star* (Poole: Javelin, 1986)

Peel, J. and Ravenscroft, S., *Margrave of the Marshes* (London: Bantam, 2005)

Romano, W., *Prog Rock FAQ: All That's Left to Know about Rock's Most Progressive Music* (London: Backbeat, 2015)

Rossi, F., *I Talk Too Much: My Autobiography* (London: Constable, 2019)

Russo, G., *Mannerisms: The Five Phases of Manfred Mann* (New York: Crossfire, 1995, 4th ed. 2022)

Thompson, D., *Cream: How Eric Clapton Took the World by Storm* (London: Virgin, 2005)

Articles and Interviews
Anon., *'Manfred's Mannerisms' (Manfred Mann and Chris Thompson interview) (Beat Magazine,* March 1978)

Ashberry, S., *'Manfreds march on' (Bradford Telegraph & Argus*, 3 April 1998)

Barkham, P., *'What Greenpeace could learn from Manfred Mann about saving the environment' (Guardian*, 5 July 2015)

Coxhill, G., *'Back to Pop: Why Manfred Has Gone Back to Pop' (New Musical Express*, 19 June 1971)

Edmands, B., *'Manfred's on the charts again', (New Musical Express*, 27 May 1978)

Fielder, H., *'The Changing Face of Mann' (Sounds*, 31 August 1976)

Jones, T., *'Messin' With Manfred Mann', (Record Collector*, March 2000)

-- *'Mann Overboard' (Record Collector*, October 2007)

Kirmser, E., *'Of Manfred Mann & Earth & Chocs,' (Rolling Stone*, 23 December 1971)

Klee, J. *'5 Generations of Manfred Mann' (Rock Magazine*, 26 Feb 1973)

Ledgerwood, M., *'Manfred Mann is alive and well, and living in a contented family life in suburbia' (interview) (Disc and Music Echo*, 2 October 1971)

Morley, S. 'Legitimate point of view' (Paul Jones interview) (*The Times*, 1 July 1982)

Neale, G. 'From Pop to Rock with Manfred Mann' (*Way Ahead*, 22 September 1976)

Petridis, A., '60s hitmakers Manfred Mann: "I've sung this 10,000 times and never liked it!"' (*Guardian*, 14 October 2021)

Plummer, M., 'Mann of the People' (*Melody Maker*, 29 May 1971)

Shindler, M., 'Manfred Mann: blinded by the spotlight' (*Rolling Stone*, April 1977)

Ward, J., 'Earth Mann' (*Melody Maker*, 30 March 1974)

Welch, C., 'Mann of the Moment' (*Melody Maker*, 11 September 1976)

Winton, B., 'Manfred Mann's Earth Band' (*Record Collector*, August 1988)

Internet

Chris Thompson interview (Cryptic Rock online, 21 July 2015) *https://crypticrock.com/*

Feenstra, P., Manfred Mann interview (Get Ready to Rock Radio, Mixcloud, February 2021) *https://www.mixcloud.com*

Fielder, H., *The story behind the song: 'Blinded by the Light' by Manfred Mann's Earth Band* (Classic Rock online, 12 February 2018) *https://www.loudersound.com/*

Jacobson, D., *Chicago In Song: Hater's Paradise* (Beachwood Reporter, 3 January 2022 *http://www.beachwoodreporter.com*

James, G., *Manfred Mann interview*, n.d. *www.classicbands.com*

Markhorst, J., *Get your Rocks Off Manfred Mann!* (Untold Dylan online, May 2020) *https://bob-dylan.org.uk*

Zimmermann, C., In Defense: Manfred Mann's Earth Band's 'Blinded by the Light' (Cover Me, 24 September 2019) *https://www.covermesongs.com*

allmusic.com
discogs.com
45cat.com 45cat vinyl database
platform-end.co.uk Manfred Mann's Earth Band Archive
youtube.com – Manfred Mann, Chris Slade, Chris Thompson interviews

Journals
Beaver County Times
Classic Rock
Disc and Music Echo
Guardian
Let it Rock
Melody Maker
Mojo
New Musical Express
Phonograph Records Magazine
Record Mirror
Rolling Stone
Sounds
The Times
Uncut

Also available from Sonicbond

Decades Series
The Bee Gees in the 1960s – Andrew Mon Hughes et al 978-1-78952-148-1
The Bee Gees in the 1970s – Andrew Mon Hughes et al 978-1-78952-179-5
Black Sabbath in the 1970s – Chris Sutton 978-1-78952-171-9
Britpop – Peter Richard Adams and Matt Pooler 978-1-78952-169-6
Alice Cooper in the 1970s – Chris Sutton 978-1-78952-104-7
Curved Air in the 1970s – Laura Shenton 978-1-78952-069-9
Bob Dylan in the 1980s – Don Klees 978-1-78952-157-3
Fleetwood Mac in the 1970s – Andrew Wild 978-1-78952-105-4
Focus in the 1970s – Stephen Lambe 978-1-78952-079-8
Free and Bad Company in the 1970s – John Van der Kiste 978-1-78952-178-8
Genesis in the 1970s – Bill Thomas 978178952-146-7
George Harrison in the 1970s – Eoghan Lyng 978-1-78952-174-0
Marillion in the 1980s – Nathaniel Webb 978-1-78952-065-1
Mott the Hoople and Ian Hunter in the 1970s – John Van der Kiste
978-1-78-952-162-7
Pink Floyd In The 1970s – Georg Purvis 978-1-78952-072-9
Tangerine Dream in the 1970s – Stephen Palmer 978-1-78952-161-0
The Sweet in the 1970s – Darren Johnson from Gary Cosby collection
978-1-78952-139-9
Uriah Heep in the 1970s – Steve Pilkington 978-1-78952-103-0
Yes in the 1980s – Stephen Lambe with David Watkinson 978-1-78952-125-2